AYLSHAM

Norfolk's premier market town, its origins & early development

by
Richard Harbord

Acknowledgements

1. A photographic aerial view of Aylsham's market place from the north-west, taken about 1900. From *'Aylsham Remembered'* ; Aylsham Town Council.
2. A drawing of Aylsham parish church by Robert Ladbrooke, made from the south-east, circa 1840. From Norfolk County Council.
3. Another aerial view of the parish church in the foreground and the market place with early cars - taken about 1920. Aylsham Town Council.
4. Photograph of Red Lion Street looking north about 1900. Aylsham Town Council
5. Tuttington Church, a drawing of the interior by John Sell Cotman. Norfolk County Council.
6. Early maps of Abel Heath & Cawston Moor. Public Record Office.
7. Battle of Hastings as shown on the Bayeux Tapestry.
8. Internal and external views of Aylsham Parish Church.
9. Early drawing of the Buttlands. Aylsham Town Council.
10. A plan of Millgate shown on the 1839 Tithe Map of Aylsham. Norfolk Record Office.
11/ 12. Two photographs of Aylsham Church.
13. Photograph of the church font.
14/ 15. panels in the medieval chancel screen of Aylsham parish church.
16/ 17/ 18, sepulchre brasses in the church.
19. a full photographical view of the chancel screen
20/ 21, Bishop Jegon's tomb and the Jermy family memorial. Corpus Christi College, Cambridge.
22. Faden's map of Norfolk – an extract showing Aylsham. Phillimore pubn.
23. Biedermann's map of the River Bure navigation – an extract showing Aylsham including Millgate. Aylsham Town Council.
25. To the Ordnance Survey who have granted a license for modern maps to be used as a base for adding historical information.

First Published 2014
ISBN 978-0-9929777-0-2

My thanks are to my wife Edith for her support and encouragement; to Jamie Nickerson who gave endless support for the computerisation of the script and images and to Lloyd Mills, the Aylsham Town Archivist. I am indebted to Dr John Sapwell for his *'History of Aylsham'* and many of the facts repeated here come from that source.
Apologies are offered in advance for any errors as these are probably inevitable given the high volume of information provided.

Printed by Barnwell Print, Aylsham, Norfolk.
www.barnwellprint.co.uk

AYLSHAM CHURCH

Frontispiece

An early history of AYLSHAM.

Preamble.

It has been rightly claimed that the study of the small market towns of Norfolk is in its infancy. If anything this is an understatement when referring to their origins. There are several thriving local history societies in the county. They find a wide public support from the nostalgia they evoke and the sense of belonging where people are proud of their roots and defensive of their locality. Society meetings tend to be gentle in dispensing information and rich in entertainment. Yet now many of these towns face serious challenges to their identity and long term well-being from over-development. One of the ways for a community to face up to these challenges is to be secure in its sense of where it came from. Only then can it know where it should be going into the long term future. This message is slow in taking hold. Prehistory ended with the birth of Jesus and history began at the same time. Since then we have had two thousand years of history yet the first millennium – half our history at a local level gets little more attention than a footnote. If we wait for the archaeologists to provide a narrative we would probably wait for a very long time. The exception has been the recent publication of '*Exploring the Norfolk Town*' by the late Christopher Barringer of the UEA in 2011. This looked at twelve towns including Aylsham in some depth but there were many leading questions about their origins left unexplored.

To approach this early time period we need a different approach to the normal way of doing history. We cannot rely on a shelf load of written references or any other sort of bibliography. We need to move to a different mode – looking at the landscape and interpreting the maps that describe it. The last part needs techniques, graphic skills, imagination etc; all the things that professional historians seem to avoid in order to be 'scientific'. We also need new rules and procedures. These are meant to serve us, not the other way round and if they do not then they should be replaced. Making statements that are 'evidence based' needs to be widened to give a lot more scope for new strategies. It is quite legitimate to place ourselves in an historical period and ask how would <u>we</u> solve their problems given the circumstances of the time. Another technique is 'backward inference' where we have an idea of what happened at a later date and assume it evolved from a previous model.

Professional historians like the late Christopher Barringer supported and advised groups of local historians helping them to get started on some of the more difficult aspects of local history. The further back we go in history the less analytical their publications became. This also needs to be reversed. It has resulted in a considerable town archive in Aylsham, Wymondham, Dereham and other places in Norfolk but there is a danger this momentum may become lost just when it should be accelerating.

This book partly attempts to up-date Dr John Sapwell's book, '*A history of Aylsham*' published in 1961, over fifty years ago. Many detailed pieces of information reproduced here come from that book but the later history (that is after the Middle Ages) is only explored for a limited number of topics and only to bring us up to the present day. Here there is no attempt to tell a comprehensive tale of the last few centuries. Many of the detail facts are summarised in the Appendices which are there for reference purposes.

1. <u>Introduction.</u>

Aylsham is only about eight miles from the north Norfolk coast. The soils are rich sandy loams left after the retreat of the last Ice Age about 12,000 years ago. They are much more fertile than the lighter soils of western Norfolk or the heavy Clay-Lands of the centre south part of the county. In north-eastern Norfolk the picture then was very mixed with many patches of very dry or very wet land, especially in the valleys. The River Bure springs from Melton Constable far to the west of Aylsham. It then the flows south-eastwards away from the Holt to Cromer Ridge; down to Blickling and Ingworth before reaching Aylsham. The main tributary streams (locally called 'Becks') flow north to south – Hagen's, Kings and Scarrow Becks before entering the River Bure. The site of Aylsham was elevated on ground slightly above the Bure Valley so wells were easily dug into the high water table. Waste water was also easily disposed of by relying on gravity. There was a combination of other natural factors that led to the beginnings of the settlement and these are what are now to be explored.

Norwich Road

Bank Street

Hungate Street

Black Boys Hotel

Town Hall

The Parish Church

Aylsham from the north-west.
The first motor cars appeared in the
market square, alongside horses.

Chapter title	Page

Images in the Preliminaries;
1. Aerial view of the Market Place taken from the church tower about 1900.
2. Robert Ladbrooke's view of the Parish Church 1820s
3. An aerial view high up above the Parish Church and Market Place about 1920
4. Red Lion Street looking northwards about 1910 – no traffic.

Red Lion Street, in the centre of Aylsham about 1900.

1. The natural landscape of north-east Norfolk.

Map 1, shows Aylsham in the context of the district that surrounds it – north-east Norfolk. In Roman times the coast was about a mile further out to sea. That is how much has been lost to erosion by the sea. The configuration of the coast can only be guessed at but it probably had a series of shallow bays and large headlands all of which have degraded over the last two thousand years. The coast was about 12 miles to the north and 11 miles north-east from the site Aylsham. From the 300 feet high sea cliffs, the land falls gently in a southerly direction. Locally the ground was much less flat than it is today with many small humps and shallow valleys – as pictured by the Romantic school of Norwich artists in the early 1800s. It was all smoothed out by industrialised farming in the following period.

Geographically this is the sandy loam, soil area of Norfolk which extends from the coast, south to Norwich; east as far as the Broads. In early history heath-land was ubiquitous across the whole district but by the late Middle Ages it had receded to a belt that stretched for fifteen miles north to south to the west of Aylsham.

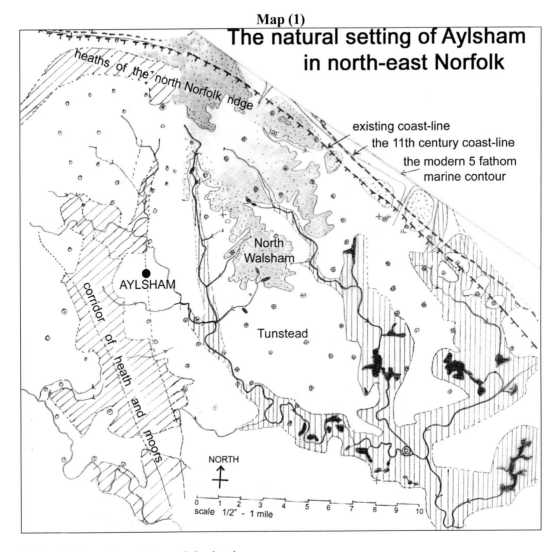

Map (1)

The natural setting of Aylsham in north-east Norfolk

existing coast-line
the 11th century coast-line
the modern 5 fathom marine contour

heaths of the north Norfolk ridge

North Walsham

AYLSHAM

corridor of heath and moors

Tunstead

NORTH

0 1 2 3 4 5 6 7 8 9 10
scale 1/2" - 1 mile

2. Pre-history; how it shaped the landscape.

In the late Stone Age the first farmers began to clear small areas of heath and woods to begin cultivation. Aylsham is on a plateau above the valley of the River Bure. The +30 metre contour runs above the river and its tributaries. The Mermaid Beck is a stream that forms the southern boundary of the present parish. The modern town centre is half a mile south-west of the River Bure. It lies on well drained land above the flood-plain and meadows of this slow flowing river. In the Early Bronze Age (2500-1250 BC) monuments were raised to the early farmers in the form of burial mounds. Most of these have been destroyed by later farming and settlement. It is only those on the perimeter of the parish that survive – in Tuttington Woods at the eastern corner of the parish boundary and 'Gay's Hill' on heath-land on the western side (see Map 2, below). Later in the Bronze Age there was a shift of emphasis from cultivation to livestock farming and that led to a need for markets, drove-ways and the formation of long distance track-ways. These required places to meet which were also used for a variety of other religious and social purposes. Most track-ways lead from the north Norfolk coast southwards to a focal place east of Norwich.

10

East-west track-ways were far less significant. Besides county-scale hubs there were also more local ones. To the east of Aylsham is one of the north-south track-ways. It led to Cromer, a fishing village previously called 'Shepden'. There, there is a low point in the cliffs that allows access to the beach and historically to inland trade on that beach. These factors favoured it above the neighbouring track-ways either side of it running through the district. The track which passed through the site of Aylsham led towards the highest point on the coastal hills – at 'Roman Camp' in Aylmerton.

The track through North Walsham also led to another high point on the coast – to Beacon Hill in Trimingham parish. The central track of this district was given priority over those either side of it from the beginning. It followed closely the western side of the Kings Beck which flows north to south. On this route and between Hanworth and Roughton is a huge assemblage of pre-historic monuments including a long barrow (rare for Norfolk) and other types of burial mound or ring burials; a wayside enclosure that could also have been a Henge etc. Later in the Iron Age a cursus or ceremonial avenue led westwards to a sacred place – perhaps a great Oak and a spring. The very name of the tribe that dominated Norfolk 'Iceni' – translates as the 'People of the (Sacred) Oak'. There may have been another assembly place in the middle of Erpingham parish two miles north of Aylsham, where there were round enclosures and more burial sites. Running through it is a mile long feature running across the track-way towards what is now the Aylsham by-pass. It is of unknown date or purpose – it may have been a defensive dyke. Another similar feature crossed the track to Cromer. This ran east and west, forming an embankment enclosing the Norman deer park between the parishes of Hanworth and Alby.

As farming evolved over two thousand years, extensive areas were being cultivated and that led to co-axial field systems in some parts of Norfolk. These are most in evidence in the Clay-Lands in southern-central Norfolk. Because of the patchwork of gravels and poor soils of north-east Norfolk, this district was less suitable for this method of landscape management. Instead there were disconnected areas of farming inter-mixed with extensive heaths. The one exception to that was the area around Happisburgh on the coast. In the Middle Ages the farmland of several parishes ran into each other. Most of pre-medieval Happisburgh has gone into the sea due to erosion but there are still crop marks in the landscape showing early field systems.

Pre-history left to us these five landscape components which influenced what happened later; farmland systems; track-ways and local defences, burials and gathering places. The component that has left no clear evidence is the landed estate of the tribal period. The only means of guessing how these estates were managed and organised is through the conservation and management of woodland (see the Appendix). Both Aylsham and Walsham later developed into estate centres from the late Anglo-Saxon period onwards and it is possible that these dated much further back into antiquity. If that was the case, it might explain why the major north-south track-way bypassed the site of the future town of Aylsham.

Map no 2, (below) shows the extent of the modern parish of Aylsham and its natural setting. The River Bure provides a strong boundary on the eastern side. The meadows that line either side of it produced a wild-life corridor in early times – the refuge for wild animals and also for bandits. There were few safe crossing points, which made the original ford north of the present town centre so important. To the west of the town there was a huge expanse of woodland – the 'Great Wood' of Aylsham that was fiercely protected by the landowners' agents. This was gradually 'assarted' and reduced in size. It degenerated into heath and then further declined into 'waste' when even some of the top-soil was taken away. This still left a huge expanse of land incapable of being cultivated – over two thousand acres of it. The west of the parish was part of the great north-south belt of moors. Where long distance routes passed through these heaths there was an opportunity for robbers and highwaymen to ply their trade. Most north-south routes avoided it and lay either side of it. That favoured Aylsham's development.

The early histories of Aylsham and North Walsham are comparable in several ways. The difference is in their urban formation. In the case of Walsham, 'common-edge' drift led to several isolated satellite groups of houses and small-holdings developing away from the town centre and clustered around a series of small commons. This is a feature frequently found in Norfolk settlements but to a much less degree in Aylsham. The town remained for most of its history focussed on the town centre. The ribbon development forming a northern suburb along Millgate Street and spreading further north to Abbott's Hall was something that occured late in its history. The town centre was nucleated within a compact area of about 80 acres and that included yards, orchards, paddocks etc attached to dwellings and businesses. The only outlying centres were the minor estates of Woodgate, Bolwick, Abbott's and Coldham Halls.

MAP (2) <u>The parish of Aylsham and the local topography</u>.

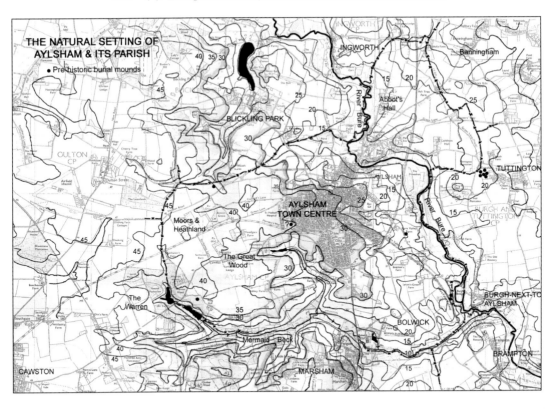

In the southern part of the parish, the River Bure flows on the eastern side sharing a boundary with Burgh-by-Aylsham. The anomaly of the parish is its northern part. There the river flows on the western side of Aylsham forming a boundary shared with Blickling. The inter-change between these two areas, north and south occurs near the bridges on

Millgate. Apart from the stream along the southern parish boundary there are no other natural geographical features. On the west and northern sides, the parish lines seem arbitrary. In pre-history there was no boundary - only a sort of 'no-mans-land' between settlements.The following map shows the extent of long distance pre-historic track-ways in the district around Aylsham. The all year round track-ways follow the inter-fluvials in a mainly north-south direction. These have already been described. There may have been an additional north-south route leading to Happisburgh; that is until the Norfolk Broads began to develop in the early Middle Ages and interrupted this track-way so it was diverted. It is worth mentioning because Happisburgh was probably the key settlement in north-east Norfolk until marine erosion reduced its territory and importance. There were few landing places for boats on the north Norfolk coast between the Yare Estuary to the east and inlets far to the west. The early shape of the coast suggests there could have been an inlet and landing place at Happisburgh. It was only after Happisburgh's status was reduced that other places in the district like Aylsham gained much local importance.

MAP (3) <u>The prehistoric landscape of north-east Norfolk.</u>

LONG DISTANCE NATIVE TRACK-WAYS IN NORTH-EAST NORFOLK

When the Romans arrived in East Anglia the rulers of the Iceni were able to call together this confederation of minor tribes because they were bound together by tribute and local ownership patterns. We don't know how this confederation operated but history tells us that the Iceni collectively coordinated their confrontation against the Roman invaders. The eastern side of Norfolk was at this time settled much less densely than the western part of the county. Archaeological finds in Aylsham show there was human activity there from pre-historic times but no evidence has yet been found of any pre-historic settlement there.

3. The Romans in north-east Norfolk - a formally planned landscape?

With the arrival of the Romans, local administration and land management was put on a much more formal basis. At the local level we can again only guess at what that implied. They took over the existing pattern of native track-ways. Where they found no effective east-west system of routes they built at least one. Its western end began at the town of *Durobrevae* on the River Nene between Stamford and Peterborough. The 'Fen Causeway' crossed into Norfolk. One route (A) seems to have continued eastwards from the Roman Fort at Billingsford to a marching camp on the northern side of Cawston, directly through Aylsham towards Happisburgh. This camp seems to have been located east of Nettleship Farm (TG14 24) and it had triple ditches. The east and west sides of the camp were not parallel; the corners were radiused – was it indeed Roman? Barringer suggested there was a shift (southwards?) from the old Roman road to a new alignment without explaining where he meant.

The early route seems to have been superseded when the fort and town south of Brampton was built. Its position was determined by being the head of navigation on the River Bure. Its site is only 2½ miles south of Aylsham. It had a huge industrial area devoted mainly to pottery production. 145 kilns have been identified on the site but only a handful of them have been investigated. Grey pot kitchen-ware and white mortaria (mixing bowls) were made. The former have been found on Hadrian's Wall which suggests much of the output shipped down the river to Caister was intended for the Roman Army. There were also wells, a temple, metal working etc in the town (its Roman name is unknown). The lozenge shaped enclosure near the old course of the river covered about 17 acres and was defended by a ditch. This was allegedly the third largest Roman town in Norfolk. This ranking is based on our ignorance of the scale of Roman Happisburgh which has largely disappeared into the sea.

Just to the north of Brampton was a Roman villa-farm. The site is in the southern part of Aylsham parish and in two places just east of Bolwick Hall. In 2014, Roman kilns were reported in a field next to Woodgate Nurseries, a mile west of the town though yet to be confirmed. Multiple other finds reported by the owner suggest this may also have been a villa of Roman-British farmstead. The only other evidence of Roman occupation in Aylsham town centre is two ditches on the east side of Red Lion Street. The ditches were filled with Roman debris such as broken pottery and roofing pantiles. The finds were noticeably of low status quality compared to the higher status finds made at Bolwick such as Samian pottery-ware imported from France. Very little other archaeological excavation has been made in the town so these finds only provides us with a glimpse of what was there in the Roman period.

The east-west Roman Road (B) to Brampton by-passed Aylsham but aerial photography of the town at Brampton suggest that a road branched northwards towards the site of Aylsham. Another branch seems to have led towards the site of Brampton village. A third northern route followed the eastern side of the Bure in the direction of Coldham Hall. Native tracks already existed so the Romans only had to up-grade them by improving their bearing course with gravel and perhaps debris from the kilns in Brampton.

MAP (4) The Roman landscape.

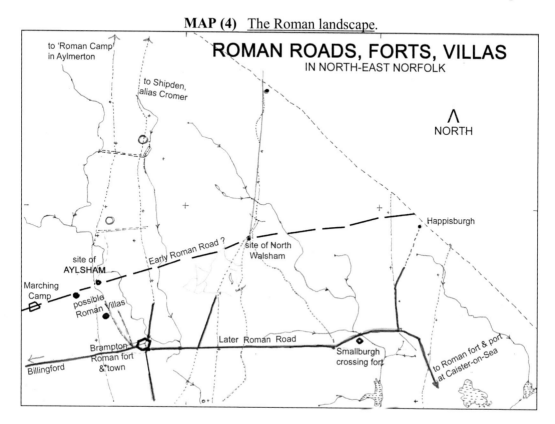

When looking at the urban geography of the town centre it is tempting to see a degree of planning in the regular geometry and even symmetry of part of the street layout inside the modern town. Even if that was the case, at what date was it laid out?

The town centre lies in a rectangular area of about 80 acres. The original north-south route seems to have passed through the centre and is reflected in the Medieval street of Hungate on the south side of the town centre. The alignment of this 'desire line' continues northwards through the burial yard of the parish church and into Cromer Road. At right angles to it on the southern side about 350 metres from the burial yard is Buttlands Lane, later called Mill Road, and Palmers Lane. On the northern side and also about 300 metres from the churchyard is Bure Way. To the west of the church yard and about 200 metres away is Pound Lane continued north as Sandy Lane. On the opposite side to the east and also 200 metres away is Oakfield Road.

Also symmetrical to this geometry are two routes radial to the church – Norwich Road to the south-east and Cawston Road to the south-west. The alignment of these roads and lanes need to be dated. Most of these main streets and lanes are shown on the 1797 survey map published by William Faden (see the Appendix). Some of them may have been recent developments. As there are no surviving earlier survey maps of the town centre it is difficult to be certain on this issue.

MAP (5) <u>The roads and streets of Aylsham.</u>

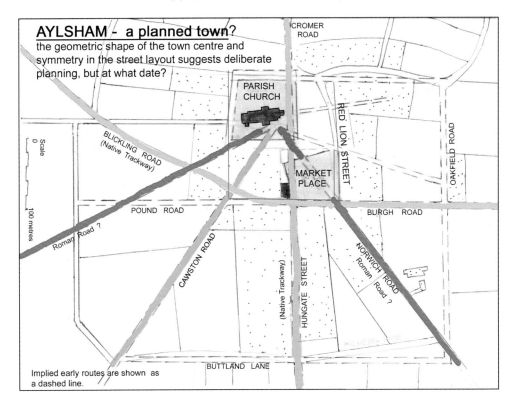

MAP (6) <u>Aylsham town centre.</u>

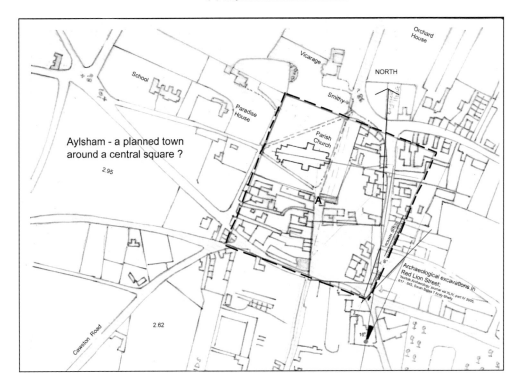

If we look closer at the town centre plan there seems to be a square area with a right-angle in the north-west corner of the medieval churchyard. This produces two sides to the square to the north and west. A third southern side to a square could be drawn along Pinfold Street - Bank Street, even though these do not now have a consistently straight road frontage. Red Lion Street has a road frontage that also varies in its alignment and this seems to defy any attempt to superimpose the fourth straight side to our town centre 'box'. If we return to the western and larger of the two Roman ditches alluded to above, we find that its angle differs from that of the present street by several degrees. In fact it then does provide us with the fourth side to our postulated urban square. The Roman content of that ditch discounts a later date for this feature.

A further feature found in 1955 was a four feet wide wall foundation west of Holman House, next to the Churchgate, marked 'A' on the plan below. No dating material is known relating to this feature – was it Medieval or much earlier? (ALHS Journal).

4. Early Anglo-Saxon period, 400-600 AD.

The close proximity of the Roman town of Brampton to Aylsham suggests that one might have been abandoned at the same time that the other was first occupied. As the demand for Roman pottery collapsed and the industrialised part of the town was full of decaying buildings there would have been a good case for moving from Brampton (meaning the 'burnt town') to a new drier site away from the river as at Aylsham. The river was navigable westwards as far as Brampton during the Roman occupation. It may have silted up by 400AD which would have been another reason for abandoning the site.

The Roman and Anglo-Saxon periods add up to half our history yet on the local level it is mostly neglected. This is partly because we call it the 'Dark Ages' because few records survive and archaeology can only give us a generalised narrative. In this period immigration from the north-western part of the continent and the colonisation of north-eastern Norfolk gathered momentum. The name 'Anglo' implies Danish, and 'Saxon' means Germanic peoples. In the previous period it was in the western part of Norfolk rather than the north-east that most of the native population lived. After 400 AD this was slowly reversed. North-eastern Norfolk was to become one of the most densely populated areas of England. There are about 120 villages in the district now, in a triangular area 30 miles east to west, and 20 miles north to south. It happened because the whole landscape was turned up-side down in a revolution greater than any other that has occurred before or since. The new settlers brought a communal form of society called feudalism. This introduced a cooperative form of agriculture so farmland could be greatly expanded and also be settled. Villages could then become nucleated settlements with a dual focus – the church and manor-house. Instead of being scattered across the landscape, burials were also centred on and usually placed within settlements. It is debatable whether this evolved slowly over several centuries based on the few villages that already existed in Roman times. There were certainly some pre-Anglo Saxon settlements in Norfolk but nothing like on the scale that developed during this period. The Romans left England in 410 AD, and two centuries later the process of settlement gathered speed. The local system of Roman governance was probably taken over by those natives who had been Romanised. The old order may have taken a century to finally disappear. It is probable that there was a long period of insecurity caused by roving bands of robbers before the settlement process could develop and flourish. It was about 600 AD that the first Christian missionaries arrived in Norfolk and that was to change everything.

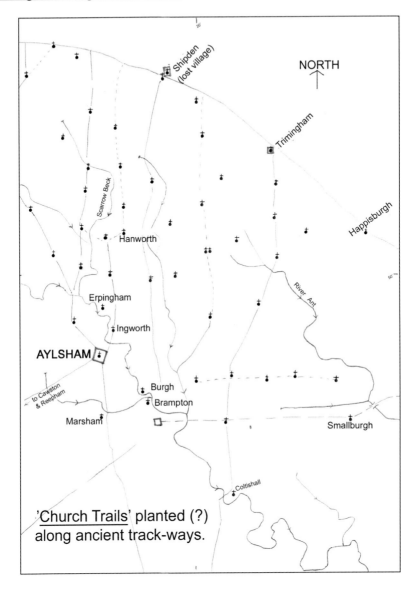

By 600 AD, a dynasty of regional rulers of Scandinavian origin settled on the southern coast of Suffolk – at Rendlesham, Snape and Sutton Hoo. They could only exact taxes from their territories by using warrior bands to demand tribute and if that was refused, the resisting settlement was probably burnt down. The new missionaries pointed to a more productive way of collecting taxes – through organising administrative areas grouping settlements together. Before they could begin this process they needed the king's permission to occupy the ruined Roman sea forts along the coast of East Anglia such as Happisburgh. From these bases they made forages into the pagan countryside to proselytise the Christian faith. Where they planted their crosses, a church was built and the village followed. What probably accelerated the process of conversion was that the angry Vikings threatened the Norfolk coast about 400 miles to the north-east and to the south-

west at an equal distance were the advancing armies of Islam. Norfolk is at the end of a peninsular of land with water on three side for a distance north-south of 60 miles so it has always been isolated from the rest of mainland England, exposed to invasion and vulnerable to attack. Geographically it is like a thumb sticking up into the North Sea. Creating settlements that were able to be self-sufficient for defence was probably a factor in their planning. It is tempting to think that the location and disposition of villages was planned by church and state working together.

Along the main north-south routes passing through north-east Norfolk there are 'church trails' located in a line and at regular intervals as the local geography allowed. This does not quite apply to Aylsham where there are few villages near to it. This is because it occupies a larger area than the average parish. It covers well over 4000 acres compared with the average parish size of 1000 - 2000 acres. Another reason was perhaps because it was from the start an important key settlement.

6. <u>Settlement patterns in north–east Norfolk.</u>

MAP (8)

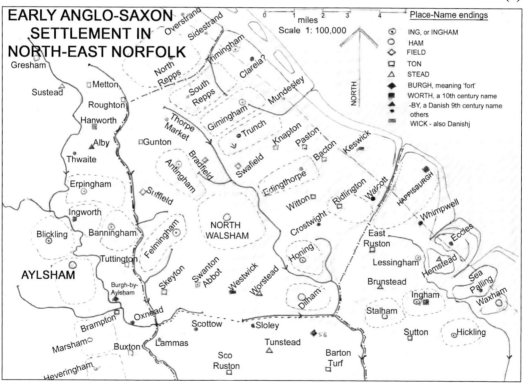

There is a mixture of 120 pre and post Viking place-names which are split almost evenly down the middle. Those places with a '*ham*'-endings clearly come within the first category – Aylsham, Reepham, Walsham etc. Those with '*ingham*' endings are the same; Trimingham, Banningham, Sheringham etc. Those with 'ton' endings are arbitrary and uncertain though they sound more Danish than Saxon. Ingworth is a hybrid name. The meaning of '*Ayl*' is either a personal forename, or its alternative meaning is lost.

We can take the search for a planned landscape a stage further by looking at the geographical context of Aylsham on a county wide scale on Map (9) below. Aylsham is located on an axis diverging from the east-west Roman Road between Bawdswell and Brampton and already referred to above as a possible early Roman Road. The axis of the 'proto-towns' directly links Bawdswell and Happisburgh. The modern road is fairly direct between the townships at its western end but further east it meanders across the landscape. It is curious that this line of towns points to the geographical centre of Norfolk; to North Elmham where the earliest Anglo-Saxon cathedral in the county was situated and the huge and very early Anglo-Saxon cremation and burial site on Spong Hill which lay just to the south of North Elmham. The trail includes Happisburgh, North Walsham, Aylsham, Cawston, Reepham and Billingford which was a Roman camp. The consistency of this trail looks to be more than just a coincidence. Whether or not this was planned remains an open question.

7. Middle Anglo-Saxon administrative boundaries.

These probably evolved from much earlier historical periods. They imply that central places acting as administrative hubs were already in place by the 'long 8th century'. This is so named because there was an acceleration of development during this period, nationally and locally. County and parish boundaries came much later in history. There were only zones of influence and authority was in a centre-place stronghold. These local areas were partly based on old loyalties, tribal boundaries and no-mans lands were often fought over by territorial magnates. It seems to imply a distinct pattern in north-east Norfolk. Later administrative units resulted from the sub-division of the earlier larger areas. The reason may have been there were far fewer established settlements and far fewer people available in the earlier pre-Viking period to administer them or to be administered. A speculative re-creation of these units is shown in Map (9).

The district fell into three possible administrative 'zones' whose generic name is now lost. The word '*Hundred*' is first heard of in England in the 7[th]c and the use of this term in the late Anglo-Saxon period could be a carry-over from the earlier period. It means a hundred plough-lands which could collectively contribute an amount of tax money equal to other districts. This method of equalising tax liability was intended to reduce disputes between different districts. Alternative administrative terms used elsewhere in England were the *lathe,* or *wapentake* but no evidence has been found of their use in north Norfolk. Each administrative area was focussed on a distinct hub settlement – the future market towns. The zone dominated by Aylsham stretched from the north Norfolk coast south to the inter-fluvial area between the rivers Bure and Wensum. Eastwards the King's Beck separates it from zone dominated by Walsham.

To the west of Aylsham was the belt of heath-land already alluded to. It was used for rough grazing so this area was probably the place of disputes between different settlements – hence the need to avoid specific boundary lines until much later in history.

This period ended with the invasion of East Anglia by the Vikings. The 'bad Vikings' suggests that they were pan-Scandinavians pagans or rather akin to pirates. The 'good' Vikings were mainly from Denmark and were more organised. When that country began to be converted to Christianity, the pagans there started to roam abroad in their long boats. Internal political divisions in England weakened its response to this threat. In 793 King Aethelbert, king of East Anglia was killed by King Offa of Mercia. Beowulf was killed in 823 and in 836 Egbert became king. Soon afterwards, the Vikings were wintering in Norfolk. By 856 Norfolk was already part of 'Dane-Law' and that was later to include all of eastern England. That was accomplished in 866 after they marched north and attacked York. In 870 they retreated from their attack on Wessex and marched from Cirencester back to East Anglia. Ivor 'the Boneless' was in Thetford in 869.

MAP (9) <u>The proto-townships between North Elmham and Happisburgh.</u>

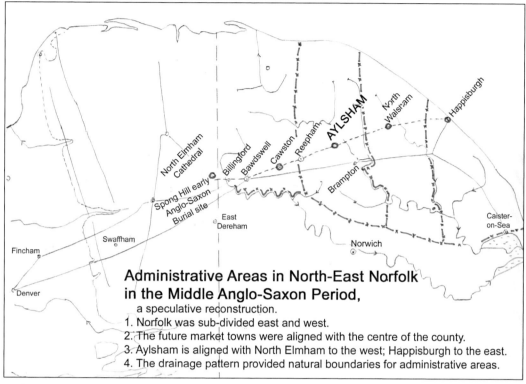

Administrative Areas in North-East Norfolk
in the Middle Anglo-Saxon Period,
a speculative reconstruction.
1. Norfolk was sub-divided east and west.
2. The future market towns were aligned with the centre of the county.
3. Aylsham is aligned with North Elmham to the west; Happisburgh to the east.
4. The drainage pattern provided natural boundaries for administrative areas.

Whether or not the location of the towns was planned or an accident remains an open question.

Edmund the last king of East Anglia and Bishop Humbert were martyred by the Danes in 870. Peace with Wessex was made in 878 in Chippenham. Religious conversion of the Danes then began but it was a very slow process.

For the most part the Vikings were pagans who ruled by natural religion and secular laws so their targets were the Christian monasteries and churches. Many villages were deserted at this time. There was no bishop or organised church in Norfolk for a century. Aylsham probably became deserted.

8. <u>Late Anglo-Saxon period, 870-1066.</u>

After the Danish leader, Guthrum met Alfred King of Wessex in Wiltshire, he was baptised. Wessex then recognised Danelaw and that allowed the recovery to begin in Norfolk. Heavy settlement by Danes in the area followed. Secular and religious recovery was very slow. The Vikings with their double headed axes liked to chops things into two. The sub-region was divided into two counties. Norfolk and Suffolk were separated along the River Waveney. The county became a new administrative entity led by a Yarl. The diocese was sort of divided but a single bishop seems to have had a base in each of the two counties. It was the sub-division of the Hundreds that most affected Aylsham.

The Danish Hundred covered a hundred plough-lands or '*carucates*' of about 120 acres. The previous administrative areas were probably based on the three proto-towns of north-east Norfolk – Aylsham, Walsham and Happisburgh. Then a great deal of new colonisation took place so there was a much bigger population by the 900s. Just as they divided the old region into two new counties they seem to have split the old administrative units into small ones north and south. In many places the new Hundreds abandoned the old river boundaries.

MAP (10) <u>The 'Hundred' boundaries in north-eastern Norfolk.</u>

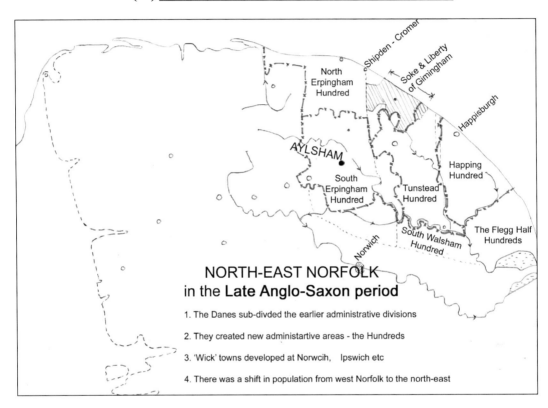

The Aylsham area was also split up into two parts. Small villages on the north-east and south-east sides of the former administrative areas seem to have been added from the former Walsham unit. Walsham was split up into its northern and southern components. The southern half of the former Happisburgh unit was sub-divided to create the two half-hundreds; East and West Flegg. Then the focal point for muster and array in civil defence were also moved. These places sometimes gave their names to the new hundreds – Erpingham is near the border of the two Hundreds. A military manorial family lived there well into the Middle Ages. 'Aylsham Hundred' (if it was previously so-named) was replaced with the Erpingham Hundreds – north and south.

The name 'Walsham Hundred' was also renamed as the 'Tunstead Hundred'. Part of these changes may have been the consequence of the destruction of those towns and their minster churches by marauding Vikings. That destruction would have reduced their effectiveness as a hub settlement. The taxation table below (Chart 1) shows that Aylsham did not stand out as a large or an important settlement in the post-Viking period; in fact just the opposite.

Chart (1)
Danish Taxation in some of the vills of the South Erpingham Hundred.

8. Danegelt **951** AD	jurisdiction area		assessments
Aylsham	2L x 2L		1s-8d
Coltishall	1½ x ½ L	1s	-
Brampton	6F x 5F		5½d
Marsham	1L 3F x 7F	11d	2s-9d
Cawston	2 L x 2L	7d	
Blickling	1 L x 1L	4½d	
Scottow	1L x ½L 2P	1s-4d	
Belaugh			1s-8d
Skeyton			1s-8d

Aylsham was just one of many vills in the Hundred even if it was at the top-end of the list in terms of size and tax paid. Only Happisburgh retained its local significance. Despite these changes, South Erpingham remained geographically the largest hundred in the district with 43 villages compared with 30 in North Erpingham. Many in the former hundred were small, fragile rural or coastal hamlets. The deciding factor was that each Hundred had to contribute an equal share of the counties taxation quota.

9) Aylsham's Area of Jurisdiction.

This is a subject that seems to have been little studied as it requires a degree of interpretation to understand it. There were at this early date no parish boundaries. Instead the manorial bailiff had the legal power to act within a zone laid down by the Sheriff and Judges. Every village had one. Its physical limits were measured exactly sometimes down to a few yards. The reason for that was that it extended either into a wilderness area or to a church door. It takes guess work usually to work out where were the four points of the square or rectangular area were. In the case of Aylsham we have a good clue because the *Domesday Survey* says that Tuttington was within this area. The River Bure became the Hundred boundary and clearly that formed the eastern limit of the jurisdiction. Tuttington lies within that boundary. The area was a large one – two leagues square. A league is 3 miles so the area extended to 6 miles on each side. The regular geometry of this area fitted in comfortably with the north-south routes in the area. It covered an area of 23,000 acres or 36 square miles. This was much bigger than the modern parish which covers about 4,300 acres. Cawston had a similar area of jurisdiction and the two over-lapped. If we try to lay Aylsham's area over the modern map on the north side it could have included the villages of Wolterton, Calthorpe, Erpingham, Colby but not Suffield which was over the border in Tunstead Hundred. On the west side there was the long distance belt of heath-land where there are fewer villages – Cawston, Oulton and possibly Itteringham may have been included in the area. To the south, are only Heveringham, Brampton and Marsham. To the east there was Colby already mentioned; Banningham, Tuttington, Burgh and perhaps also Oxnead. The total number of villages was therefore 12 to 14 villages within the orbit of Aylsham.

Some local historians have pointed to a feature on the map that occurs in several parts of Norfolk. This is the radial pattern of Medieval parish boundaries. Several Norfolk towns are surrounded by parishes whose boundaries seem to radiate from the town's centre. North Walsham is a good example with nearly 20 villages falling into that description. (See the map in the Medieval section – Chapter 15). In the case of Aylsham the pattern is not so obvious until we study the area of jurisdiction. The reason for this system was that someone accused of a serious crime had two choices – to submit to the manorial court where local feuds might prejudice their case; or make a run for it. A hue and cry would then follow but if fugitives could reach the 'sanctuary ring' on the door of a neighbouring church they were safe for forty days before summary justice was delivered.

MAP (11) <u>The village bailiff's territorial limit of authority.</u>

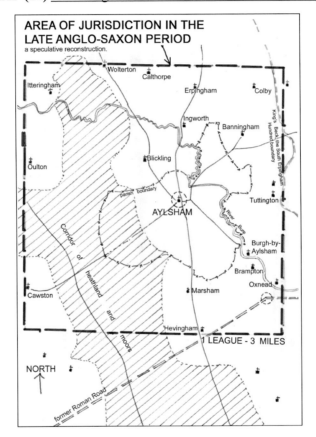

An example of a sanctuary ring can be seen in a drawing made by the Norfolk artist John Sell Cotman in 1822. It shows the medieval south door of Tuttington Church (see below). The door was planked and barred with heavy iron studs. It had elaborately crafted iron work and the ring itself was in the centre. It was probably in poor shape in 1822 and the Victorians replaced it with a new door. The original is now lost. The Bailiff of the Hundred also had jurisdiction over Aylsham even though it was a royal manor. The Hundred of South Erpingham sometimes met at the same place used by the neighbouring Hundreds of North Erpingham and Tunstead – that is at a place on the northern end of the Antingham Ponds. Usually moots met at a great burial mound but not in this case. This site may have been where the River Ant sprung in a sacred spring and a great Oak tree grew but that is speculation.

IMAGE (1) Tuttington Church door

14.75' x 10.75' drawing by John Sell Cotman
in chalk.
TUTTINGTON CHURCH - interior view
11 November 1841

Tuttington Ch(urch)
Nov . 11ᵗʰ 1841

Door given to(...)
B(...)pure, B(...) o(...)

Key plate on the centre
of the church door

Elaborate poppyhead
bench-end with carved
figures and finials - late
medieval.

Sanctuary Ring in the
centre of the door panel

10. <u>The early status of Aylsham</u>.

This is difficult to guess. One clue is in the tax rate for which the town was assessed. At 20d in the £, this was one of the highest in South Erpingham Hundred but there were several other places near the town with an equal rating such as Blickling.

As a hub village Aylsham may have had an early minster church. King Canute visited the region soon after he had consolidated his hold over the region in 1020 AD. He was the son of the raging Viking 'Blue Tooth' who was an avowed pagan and had destroyed so much of the infra-structure of the region. His son Canute had married the great Queen Emma (our greatest?) from Normandy. Emma was a Christian who wanted to develop the English Church into a national institution. At that time the only great minster churches in East Anglia were on the edges of the Fens and in the southern extremity of the region. Canute and Emma wanted to nurture back into life the lesser minsters like Aylsham. This was the beginning of the future 'town church'. To differentiate it from a village church it was probably given a cruciform plan when it was first built though no evidence for this survives in the present fabric.

Aylsham Church now has a long nave, two short transepts, a chancel at the crossing and a short sanctuary. In the late Anglo-Saxon period, all churches were built with wooden or clay-lump walls and thatched roofs. Carpentry was then at its zenith – but only as long as there was a plentiful supply of building timber. Churches could be very decorative; elaborately carved like the Scandinavian 'Stave Churches' or white plastered with colourful wall patterns. The ground plan of one such church was found by archaeologists almost intact in the castle ditches of Norwich.

The scarcity of priests meant hub churches operated collegiately sending their priests out to the surrounding villages. Towards the end of this period in the mid to late 11ᵗʰc the 'Great Rebuild programme' began in Norfolk when the wooden walls of the churches were gradually replaced with stone. That meant using flints gathered in fields or on the coast. Corner stones were built of brown stones called 'conglomerates', or 'ferricrete'. This building material has a rough texture so it cannot easily be carved. It was the only building stone that was locally available. Its use in north-east Norfolk is distinctive to this historical period. Although the 'Great Rebuild' was not an event that was documented, the evidence is there to see in the fabric of many churches across north-east Norfolk. Four great magnates drove the project forward – Queen Emma; Stigand the bishop of Norfolk and later Archbishop of Canterbury; William his brother who succeeded him as Bishop of Norfolk and the Earls of Norfolk. Any distinctive stone-work from this early building phase was swept when Aylsham parish church was rebuilt in the Middle Ages.

11. Advances in agriculture.

In the Anglo-Saxon period, large open fields were held in common by the whole community and therefore farmed collectively. Labour was enforced by the manorial code as a service to the village that was accounted for in the manor court, presided over by the lord of the manor. In the case of Aylsham it remained a royal manor administered by a resident bailiff through most of its history. There were the usual three main fields – east, west and north which were farmed on a rotation basis. This could well have been an enlargement of earlier archaic field systems. Aerial photography has not to the writer's knowledge provided crop marks of early field boundaries so we have no means of confirming that. The East Field extended up to the corridor of river meadows which formed the eastern boundary of the parish. If Norwich Road was its western boundary, the field was up to ¾ mile wide. That gave it a total area of about 700 acres.

There was a water mill at the northern extremity of the East Field in Millgate. This was the 'Kings Mill' which is still there but with a much later and grander building. The East Field of Aylsham was about a mile north to south, depending where the boundary shared with Bolwick Manor began. The Field appears to have been subdivided into 14 furlongs with another four in Bolwick. These have a decided east-west alignment though they curve with the contours of the topography. Bolwick had its own small water-mill which is also still there on the southern edge of the estate.

The West Field extended south to the meadows of the Mermaid Beck which forms the south boundary shared with Marsham parish. Mary's Beck may have formed a western boundary to part of this field as far north as Woodgate Hall and the Great Wood. This suggests that the area further west of that line was used as a sheepfold even after the end of the Middle Ages. One reason for this was that it was a long way from a water-mill which seems to have been a factor in determining the shape and location of open fields. Between the eastern boundary formed by Norwich Road and the Great Wood on the western side there was probably a similar area covered by the East Field. That depended on how far north it went.

The extent of the North Field is more difficult to determine. The western half of the northern boundary of Aylsham is shared with Blickling so the West Field seems to have extended up to that boundary. Several manors seem to have overlapped in the area of Millgate at least later in the parish's history if not earlier. At this early date the cultivated area north of the Bure was limited in size perhaps to only 300 acres or half the size of the other two Fields. This encourages us to think that part of the North Field lay south of the River so then the three Fields were more evenly balanced in size.

The 'North Croft' is mentioned in 17th century documents. Did this mean that it was north of the town? It seems to have been a different area to 'Aylsham Nether Hall Manor' which was located around the Vicarage of that date and independent of the North Field. This small Vicars Manor had its own water-mill just south of Abbott's Hall. It was shown in a survey of Blickling made in 1729 – see map below. This Mill was on the north side of Millgate. It only features in the early Church Terriers as a 'piece of waste common' next to the river' suggesting that the mill had fallen into disuse soon after the 1729 survey had been made.

At the western end of the parish today there are two small lakes either side of the Cawston road. In the West Field near its centre is a smaller stream (Mary's Beck) flowing south into the Mermaid. A track crossed it by Kettle Bridge. It is difficult to know whether the area or part of it to its east of the beck – some 500 acres, was also included in the West Field.

Map (12) The Anglo-Saxon Fields of Aylsham.

Medieval open fields & furlongs in AYLSHAM

a speculative reconstruction based on later field patterns
R. Harbord, Gunton 2014

It seems to have had a total of 9 to 15 furlongs, also on an east-west alignment like in the East Field. Some idea of the later proportions of the fields come from the number of 15th century 'Tofts' – 62 in Aylsham Lancaster Manor; 44 in Aylsham Wood Manor and 9 in the Aylsham Vicarage Manor.

12. Trackways and field paths.

Maps 13 and 14, below are the earliest of any surveys of the lanes and paths leading to the parish boundaries of Aylsham. The maps survive because they related to legal disputes and served as evidence in court. One of these disputes resulted in the biggest and most comprehensive survey made for the Aylsham Duchy Manor in 1622. The following historical Map (13) shows an area on the boundary shared between Aylsham and Cawston.

Map (13)

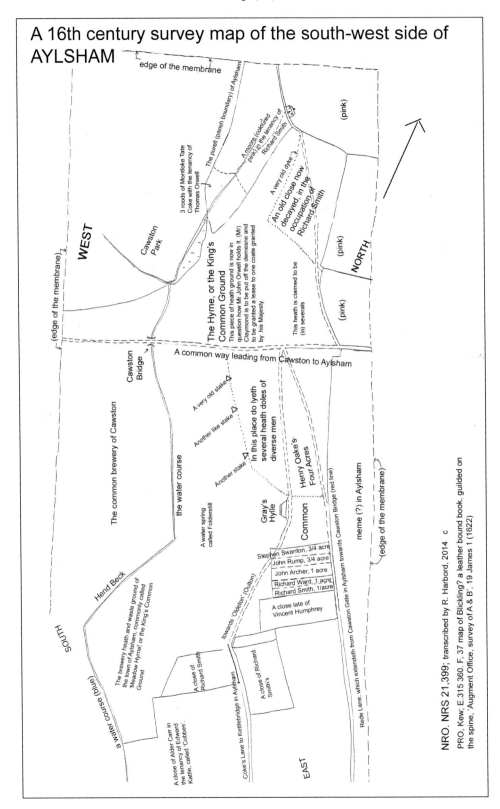

Map (14)

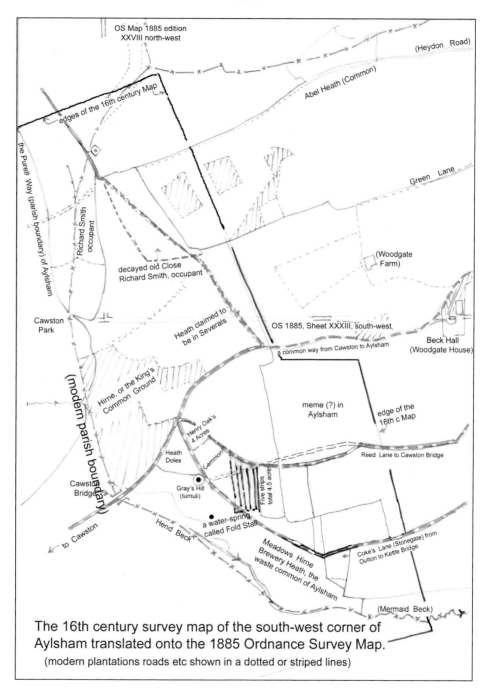

OS Map 1885 edition
XXVIII north-west

(Heydon Road)

Abel Heath (Common)

edges of the 16th century Map

Green Lane

the Purell Way (parish boundary) of Aylsham

Richard Smith occupant

decayed old Close
Richard Smith, occupant

(Woodgate Farm)

Cawston Park

Heath claimed to be in Severals

OS 1885, Sheet XXXIII, south-west

Beck Hall
(Woodgate House)

a common way from Cawston to Aylsham

(modern parish boundary)

Hirne, or the King's Common Ground

meme (?) in Aylsham

edge of the 16th c Map

Henry Oak's 4 Acres

Heath Doles

Common

Reed Lane to Cawston Bridge

Cawston Bridge

Gray's Hill (tumuli)

Five strips total 4.5 acres

a water-spring called Fold Stall

to Cawston

Hend Beck

Meadows Hirne
Brewery Heath, the
waste common of Aylsham

Coke's Lane (Stonegate) from
Oulton to Kettle Bridge

(Mermaid Beck)

The 16th century survey map of the south-west corner of
Aylsham translated onto the 1885 Ordnance Survey Map.
(modern plantations roads etc shown in a dotted or striped lines)

The map above (14) shows the same area as (13) but placed on a modern map base for the purposes of comparison.

On the north side of the parish, tracks radiated northwards from the town bridge. This pattern was disrupted by the canalisation of the River Bure and the industrialisation of Dunkirk and Drabblegate in the 19th century, so the fork in the roads was moved further north. Four ways led to the north and north-east. A fifth way led east skirting the meadows of the Bure and towards Tuttington. A total of 16 routes radiated from the centre of Aylsham. Besides these routes there were many footpaths and field-ways which did not always follow the edges of field furlongs and often crossed them between growing seasons. They were especially numerous on the margins of the parish.

Roads, tracks and paths radiating out from Aylsham across the parish;

1. Heydon Lane which continues into Aylsham and Cuckoo Lanes; with Brabon Ride forming the 'purrell way' on the northern boundary.
2. Pound, Milbourne and Codlings Lanes; a continuation of the same road that terminated at the western end at Great Wood.
3. Green Lane branching from Pound Lane. It led into Sankence Lane which turns south to join;
4. Woodgate Lane that branches south to form Cawston Road.
5. Stonegate that turned west at Abbey Farm to become Sheepfold Lane.
6. Spa Lane that skirts the southern limit of the extended West Field.

Map (15)

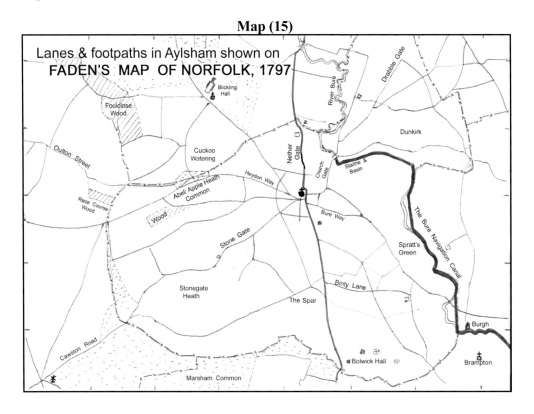

Map (14) below shows Able Heath is on the north boundary of Aylsham shared with the Silvergate part of Blickling Parish. This seems to have been another place where disputes arose around competing rights to dig for peat, extract gravel etc. Hence the survivasl of another legal document.

MAP (16) <u>Able Heath</u>

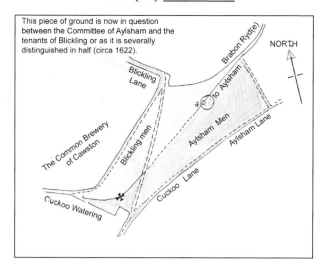

This piece of ground is now in question between the Committee of Aylsham and the tenants of Blickling or as it is severally distinguished in half (circa 1622).

13. <u>End of the Anglo-Saxon period.</u>

What did the Anglo-Saxon church of Aylsham look like? In 1040 the 'Rotunda' was built next to the Benedictine abbey church of Bury St Edmunds. It became a sepulchre shrine holding the relics of that saint and was designed in the high Carolingian style – one of the few buildings in East Anglia to aspire to such a high status in art. Pilgrims poured in from all corners of the region to see their patron saint. The roundness of the Rotunda inspired the many round bell-towers added to local churches in the region from around 1060 onwards. Perhaps the original church of Aylsham also had one as does Tuttington, Ingworth, Brampton and others nearby. This was one of the very few high status monuments in East Anglia. To a large extent the region was a cultural back-water but it had the advantage that apart from Viking attacks on the major towns, national events and upheavals by-passed the northern part of the region.

IMAGE (2)
<u>The Bayeux Tapestry and the Battle of Hasting, 1066.</u>

Aelfgar was one of the later Danish Earls of Norfolk. He was followed by Gyrth Godwinson. In 1053 Gyrth became the Earl of Norfolk and also the owner of Aylsham manor. He was the younger son of the family whose father was the Earl of Essex and had amassed large estates across England which made this the most powerful family in the land. Gyrth owned 204 estates mainly in north-eastern England including the capital manors of Aylsham, Tuttington, Wickmere, Brampton, Hevingham, Irmingland, Itteringham and Oxnead. In 1055 he was forced into exile in Flanders with the rest of his family. He was in Rome when Edward the Confessor made peace with him and his brother Harold in 1061. Harold inherited the Crown and Gyrth was with him at the battles of Stamford Bridge and

31

Hastings. Then Gyrth was allegedly killed in 1066. Both of them feature in the Bayeux Tapestry.The scene shown above allegedly shows Gyrth fighting on foot and being slain by William the Conqueror on the right who seems to have dismounted from his horse.

Although the extent of Gyrth's Norfolk estates sounds impressive, he had a powerful neighbour to the east of Aylsham. It covered about 30,000 acres and was owned by St Benet's Abbey. Whereas they made the centre for their estate management in North Walsham, the royal estates were focussed on Aylsham. It was later to become the capital manor for the royal estates in the whole of East Anglia; that is to say Norfolk, Suffolk and Cambridgeshire. At the conquest in 1066 the royal estates reverted to the Crown but William I, re-granted it to a new Earl of Norfolk, Ralph Guader the 'Staller'. He was the seignior of Gael and Montfort, and Baron of Brittany where he owned huge estates. He died in 1075 and was succeeded by his young hot-headed son the 2nd Earl, Ralph Guader, junior. He married Emma the daughter of William FitzOsborn, Earl of Hereford. Ralph also held off the king, Cawston, Marsham and Blickling. Reepham was then a small village with a jurisdiction area of only ½ league by 4 furlongs. Ralph rebelled in Norwich Castle in the same year, 1075. The king sent Roger Bigot to besiege the city and Guader fled into exile back in Brittany where he lived until 1101. Bigot then set about persecuting Guader's followers and that led to the burning and demolition of half the houses in Norwich. Guader's followers on his other estates were also persecuted. It is uncertain how this affected Aylsham.

In Norfolk, the native Saxon culture persisted long after the Norman Conquest – this is called the 'Saxo-Norman over-lap' period. Most of the Anglo-Saxon manorial lords also carried on because the great magnates like Gyrth had been largely absentee owners. It was not until the great monumental buildings of the Normans such as cathedrals and castles took shape in the 1120s that Romanesque culture began to take over.

14. The *Domesday* Survey of 1086.

This was a tax survey of the whole kingdom which was prepared for the new king, William the Conqueror. The survey covered most of England and it began in Norfolk. It was there that information was recorded in the most detail. It covered three periods – 'before' (1066); 'then' (in 1066) and 'now' (1086). All of Aylsham was included in the manor of the king.

There were 11 *carucates* with Villagers who had risen in number from 20 to 65. There were another 6½ *carucates* with 60 freemen who had been reduced to 46; 17½ *carucates* in all – a huge area of about 2100 acres. There was a large area of pig-woodland for 400 – 300 pigs. That was the equivalent of 400 – 300 acres. There is clearly a lot of meadow around Aylsham but only 21 acres were held in demesne so only they were listed as taxable. There was perhaps another 500 acres of meadow at least though it may still have been wilderness then. Out of a parish area of 4,300 acres this gives a total of 2, 520 - 2,420 acres listed.

Altogether there were 193 to 184 men. Calculating on the basis of 4½ people per man (a standard ratio) this gives an approximate population of Aylsham of 870 - 830 people. The two mills are mentioned twice – perhaps this was a repetition as only two water mills are known in Aylsham. The value of this important and large manor was £12 before; £25 'then' and £29 'now' in 1086. The big increase came in 1066. Six outlying estates were added to the capital manor of Aylsham – Stifkey, East Beckham, Shipdham, Brundall, Little Barningham and Crackford.

CHART (2)   The Great Survey or, *Domesday* entry for Aylsham, 1086.

1. 91; <u>King's Estate</u>, **Stifkey** is an outlier that belongs to the manor of Aylsham.

1.149; Siward Bairn's tenancy in **East Beckham** was added by Ralph (Guader 2nd Earl of
    Norfolk) to the manor of Aylsham.

1.192; Gyrth held Aylsham before 1066 with 16 carucates of land, then (before 1066)
    20 Villagers, now 65
    then and later (after 1066) 88 Small Holders, now 65.
    then and later, 2 servants; now 3. Then 6 ploughs in lordship; now 1; The 6 ploughs
    should still be there.
    12 acres of Meadow; then a 400 pig Wood; now 300; always 2Mills.
    Always 7 pigs, 6 sheep, 7 goats (in lordship);
    then and later, 60 Freemen, now 46, with 1½ carucates of land; 6 ploughs;
    14 Small Holders then with 30 ploughs; now with 24;
    9 acres of Meadow; a 12 pig wood; always 2 Mills.
Shipdham is an outlier to Aylsham
Brundall also appertains to this manor (of Aylsham) with 30 acres of land (etc).
    Value then £12; blanched now at £29, with a blanched premium at 20s. Tax 20d.

    The (jurisdiction of the) manor has 2 Leagues by 2 Leagues.

1.194, **Little Barningham** is in the valuation of Aylsham.

1.195, **Crackford** with 1 Freeman of Gyrth's and 1 carucate of land;
    always 3 Small Holders with 1½ ploughs then, now 1;
    2 acres of Meadow; now 1 Mill; this is in the valuation of Aylsham, tax 4d.

8.8; <u>Earl of Surrey's estate.</u>
    Tuttington was in the jurisdiction of Aylsham before 1066.

<u>Summary</u>
Total area of the capital manor in Aylsham, 16 carucates x 120 = 1,920 acres, 3050 yards
square.
Area of jurisdiction, 2 by 2 Leagues = 6 x 6 miles = 23,040 acres
Area of the medieval parish = 4,300 acres
Total pig woods – 312 acres. Total Meadows, 21 acres
Total number of men, 193 (in, 1066)--- › 184 (1086)
Total population, 193 to 184 x 4.5 (per family) = 868 – 828 people.
Mills, total 4 (or are two Mills, listed twice?)

The seven outlying parishes belonging to the capital manor of Aylsham were;
Stiffkey, East Beckham, Shipdham, Brundall, Tuttington, Crackford, Little Barningham.
Tuttington was taken out of Aylsham after 1066;
East Beckham was added after 1066.
Value of Aylsham, before 1066; £12, after 1066 - £25; in 1086, £29.

This may account for the initial rise in value. The increase in value between 1066 – 1086 was much smaller. The number of ploughs indicated in Aylsham is curious – six demesne ploughs which 'should have been there' but were not. Freemen with another six ploughs and small-holders with 30, and 'now', 24; an extraordinary large number.

Is there any evidence that the manor of Aylsham had suffered following the rebellion of its over-lord in 1075? Between 1066 and 1086 there was a minor fall in the size of the overall population and the number of Freemen but that is all. North Walsham increased in value in that period by 50% - far more than in Aylsham. This is slender evidence to support the idea that the latter was persecuted by the new Earl, Roger Bigot.

15. Medieval Manorial History.

1156, Henry II assigned the profits of the Aylsham manor together with Cawston to his brother Prince William for life, for 'his honour and support'.

Richard I, separated the capital manor or royal 'soke' into two parts. He granted the part of Aylsham north of the river to the Abbey of Bury St Edmunds. It was subsequently appropriated by the Sacristan of the Abbey so it became known as 'Sexton's Manor', and after the dissolution of the monasteries, as 'Wood Manor'. This was composed of 10 virgates of land. A '*virgate*' was a quarter of a *carucate*, (about 30 acres) so the total was approximately 300 acres. The current size of that part of the parish is a much larger area which suggests only its southern section was then farmed.

1190c; Richard I, acknowledged that the principle estate granted to Bury St Edmunds Abbey was separate from its appendage in the southern part of the parish; Bolwick. William Bardolf held the latter for a rent of 100 sols and paid another 100 sols for other land in Aylsham. The Abbey seems to have farmed out their land to John (de Hastings?) the priest of Aylsham; Hugh, dean of Ingworth; Peter de Calthorpe and 26 other tenants. Part of their rent was to provide candle-lights in the parish church for the martyr St Thomas (à Becket?) The abbot was then asked to pay *tallage* (a charge for driving beasts over a bridge) of 30s-3d. This was a tax levied by several Norman and Angevin kings across England. Much later in 1333 the abbot asked to be exonerated from the tax.

1190 King Richard went on crusade to the Holy Land and Eustace de Neville was given the Manor of Aylsham. The court only acknowledged claims to property in Aylsham where the occupants could produce their written grants. Those tenants without them lost their lands. John de Grey then claimed that he held Aylsham with Sheringham for 12d per annum paid on Lammas Day and 1 Knights Fee (garrison duty in Norwich Castle).

1199, at the death of King Richard, Eustace was still farming the manor. The new King, John directed the Sheriff of Norwich to issue a writ to transfer possession to Baldwin de Ayre. King John confirmed the settlement of the northern part of Aylsham made by his brother Richard to Abbot Sampson of Bury. By then William Bardolf and John de Hastings were the principle tenants.

1266, Henry III gave Aylsham Manor, with Cawston to Hubert de Burgh, Earl of Kent for life. The tenants protested that they had been sold land already in the multiple occupation of other people living in Aylsham.

1274, Edward I, settled the manor on his Queen, Isabella with the income from the Hundreds of North and South Erpingham.

1285, the abbot had frankpledge in Sexton's Manor for assize of bread and ale; free warren and the cost of providing a ducking stool, presumeably in the River Bure but in 2 feet of water? Every village then had its gibbet, stocks and whipping post.

1296, Edward I, held it directly with Sheringham. Richard Caly was his resident bailiff and hence 'Caly's Manor' which is a name that sometimes occurs in the records. Caly lived in a manor-house where Bolwick Hall now stands. Caly took John Holingay to court for not paying a rent of 4s-11d and fulfilling his post as the reeve for Aylsham market and the King's Mill. It was noted that all the tenants of the abbey had to grind their corn in the Abbot's mill. Was this the water-mill on the river north of Aylsham bridge later called the Vicar's Mill?

1334, a tenant in Aylsham, Agnes Smith paid 4d/ acre/ year for 14 acres of arable land; 3½d/ acre/ year for 1¼ acres of Meadow; nothing for part of a fold-course (on common land?). When the moment of decision in court was made to grant this, the abbot threw down to the floor his rod of office as was his strange custom.

1372, Edward III gave the manor to his youngest son, John of Gaunt (*Ghent*) who had inherited the title Duke of Lancaster through his wife. From then onwards Aylsham was part of the Duchy estates and indeed its capital manor from which it administered its estates in the counties of Eastern England. It became the 'Aylsham Lancaster Manor'.

1428, Sexton's Manor was valued at £27 per annum which was paid to the abbey. This figure soon dropped to £20.

1536, the monasteries were dissolved and their properties were sequested by the Crown including Aylsham Sexton's manor.

1546, 20th May, Edmund Wood bought Sextons Manor for £516-15s-2d; an annual rent of 55s-8½d and a 40th part knight fee. The sale by the Crown was confirmed by a letter patent issued under the Great Seal of State.

1548, Edmund Wood died and was succeeded by his son Robert (born in 1526) who became Mayor of Norwich in 1578.

1588, he gained a license to lease the manor to a Mr Wolmer and others.

1598, another lease was granted to a Mr Might. A Thomas Wood was still Lord of the Manor in the early 1700s. By then Sexton's Manor was known as 'Aylsham Wood Manor'. This should not be confused with Aylsham's Great Wood on the south western side of the parish.

There was still 30½ acres of woodland in Wood Manor including 28 acres in Sexton's Wood; 1½ acres in Old Wood Cop; 1 acre in Alder Carr. In these there were 400 Oaks of 40, 60 and 80 years growth – clearly planted for cropping. 200 were reserved for buildings and fences. The other 200 were valued at 4d each. Sexton's Field was north of the river but some of its tenements were in Millgate on the south side.

By custom the tenants of each of the Aylsham Manors were free from paying a series of archaic dues, across the whole of England. These eight dues were listed as;
tallege, carriage, pesage, picage, forage, pavage, lastage, stallage.

The manorial tenants of Aylsham were also free from serving in courts and on juries outside Aylsham. Sexton's/ Wood Manor extended into seven other parishes according to the **1542** custumal record (NRO, NRS 12,403; 27 DI page 5) so their annual Court Barons must have been long, drawn out and complicated affairs. Wood Manor held four courts each year;

1. An assize court for misdemeanours and a leet, on Monday before St Michael's feast.
2. A toft court to hear issues related to land and property was held on the Monday before the feast of St Agnes the Virgin.
3. Another assize court held on Whit or Low Monday.
4. Another toft court held on the 'feast of St Peters at bonds'. This manor had 44 'tofts' –

'Toft' is a Scandinavian word meaning a messuage of land/s with a dwelling attached to it. This is in contrast to the 'tenement' which was rented land with or without buildings on it. It was only later in history that a tenement was understood to be a house in multiple occupation and often of poor quality. The '*heriots*' (a fine paid to the manor when a tenant died, and paid in the form of his best beast or chattel) were certain but copyholders from outside of Aylsham paid 10s annual rent instead of 2s-8d. This manor by the late Middle Ages spread into many adjacent parishes but cases before the court often involved just one property held in free '*socage*' (ie free from feudal manorial service). Exemptions were made in the case of widows and 'chaste copy-holders' who were given 'dower'; or 'free bench'. Another strange custom was where copy-hold was imposed on each property. For every ancient messuage, one of its tenants had to go to the '*purrell*', or boundary of the leet (parish boundary?) at an appointed time perhaps to inspect what was happening there. **1660c**, one tenant, Elizabeth Brady was appointed bailiff of the manor. She employed a deputy but he could not make up the rental account of the manor so her copyhold lands were seized in a proclamation made by the manorial court.

1200c, <u>Bolwick Manor</u> was given by King John to Hugh de Burgh (Bovers?) for a ¼ knights fee. He sold it to Henry de Bolwick who gave his name to the manor. It was then recorded as having a manor house and water-mill. After a long period of ownership, the Whitwell family were still in possession in 1297.
1381 Sir Richard de Salle, of Bolwick was killed by the rebels during the Peasants Revolt. He left this manor to his wife Frances. She left it to her nephew Sir William de Trusett.
1420, Sir John Heveringham and others owned it.
1429, they sold it to William Paston and his wife Agnes (who was the daughter of Sir Edmund and his wife, Alice Burgh). The Paston family had still not yet acquired Oxnead which later was to become their main seat. When Robert Jegon surrendered this manor in c1654 it extended into Marsham. The later and successive owners of Bolwick Manor were;
Thomas Wood who married Eleanor Eyre of Derbyshire and had a daughter Mary, Mrs Suffield. Circa 1800 it was sold to the Warnes family who owned it until about 1885 when it was sold to Mr W. S. Calvert and then to a Louis Buxton.

1090c, <u>Aylsham Vicarage Manor</u> under the priest, Brithric was granted to Battle Abbey in Sussex by William II, with the church advowsons of Stiffkey, Shipdham, Brundall, Banningham; and half of Ingworth with 1 freeman. The rector and later the vicar retained a third of the great tithes; all the small tithes and the manse. Battle Abbey kept the rest of the income. At the dissolution the Bishop of Norwich became the patron who presented clergy. By the 1700s there were 30 tenants and the great tithes of Stonegate were paid to this manor. It is curious that this last item was separately singled out. Copy-holders had become free tenants only by the late 1800s. It is difficult to reconcile this large number of tenants with the smaller lists given in the 18[th]c church terriers. The latter describe a number of people living in the alms houses located mainly in lower Millgate.

The main part of this manor was called '<u>Aylsham Nether Hall</u>' as it was described in the records (see the Appendix). This was a rectangular piece of land sub-divided into nine parts, including the Parsonage in the south-eastern corner. The land was bound by Rawlinson Lane (west), Peterson Lane (north), Churchgate/ Cromer Road (east) and the churchyard (south). This was not part of the Aylsham Lancaster Manor in the 1622 schedule of land and property. In the 1839 Tithe Map Schedule (seen on page 98);

Items 7 -11, were occupied by Thomas Rackham in the north-east corner.
   12 - 14, by the Reverend Samuel Peterson
   15 – 16, by the Vicar of Aylsham.
1547, a large amount of land in Aylsham owned formerly by Thetford Monastery was sold for;   £966   15s-11d. It is unclear where this land was located.

16. Customs of the manor.
Only one '*ession*' (excuses for not appearing in the manorial court) was allowed for each tenant in all '*plaints*' (complaint or grievances aired in court) except for land issues where 3 '*essoins*' were allowed.
1304, Edward I, granted the tenants of Sexton's Manor freedom from having to plead a case outside the Abbot's court.
1422c, temp Henry VI, Lord Bardolf was the chief steward of the Duchy Court with John Payne as his under-steward. There was no resident administrative staff other than those provided by this and other magnates. This suggests there was also no permanent office in Aylsham.

17. The Market Place.

When the site of two former pubs at the southern end of Red Lion Street were recently excavated, archaeologists found evidence of general human activity going back to the late Stone Age. No evidence was found of any actual dwelling on the eastern side of the street earlier than the 11th century. That suggests that the first settlement in Aylsham was within the square area suggested above and on the western side of the town centre.
   The original market area and burial space around the parish church were one and probably not demarcated into separate functional areas. This area may have extended southwards as far as the present Town Pump. That lies at the junction of Cawston Road (SW), Blickling Road (NW), Cottage Loke (N) and Pinfold Street. In the 1622 survey of Aylsham Lancaster Manor there is a reference to the 'Old Market'. Some analysts suggest this was located in a field further north, rather than the area around the Pump. The present 19th century Pump has an open thatched roof perhaps similar to the original Cross in the later market place. The land between the Church and Pump was partly filled in when a Medieval manse and perhaps other houses were built there. This probably precluded the expansion of the existing market space and its relocation further west.
1175, the Statute of Winchester demanded that markets were taken out of churchyards and the latter were enclosed with a fence or wall. This resulted in new market places being allocated as specific places and planned in many market towns of Norfolk. Before the market place was laid out there may have been a street on its western side with houses lining both sides. This street would have been a continuation northwards from Hungate Street but that is purely speculation. It is difficult to imagine how a large new urban space could be created without conflicting with existing property rights and their curtilages to say nothing about the cost of displacing existing buildings. By owning most of the property in the town centre, the Aylsham Lancaster Manor had an advantage. Also timber-framed buildings are more easily dismantled than stone walled houses.
1274-5, Aylsham was granted a license to hold a market. This charter only recognised what had been in existence for about a century, validating an established practice. The Crown gained an income from its licensing power and the manorial lord from stallage and other dues. It is curious that the charters of Foulsham, Cawston, Reepham all pre-date the

charter for Aylsham. Other small places nearby like Burgh were granted licenses but those markets lapsed. Only a few markets in Norfolk like the one in Aylsham, flourished.

Maps (17) & (18) The compact town centre in the 19th century.
Aylsham town centre, 1885 - the earliest Ordnance Survey Map

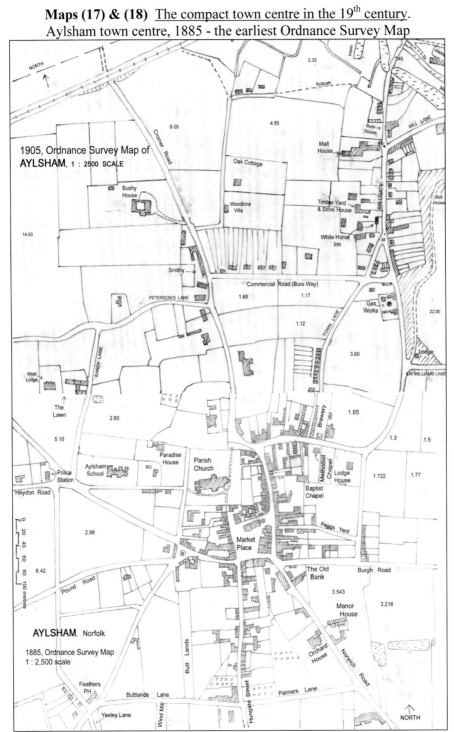

Layout of Aylsham town centre in 1839 (from the Tithe Map, NRO).

The 1622 Duchy survey of its manor in Aylsham shows stalls and shops which collectively had a frontage of about 200 feet long. Many of the stalls were only the size of a domestic dining table. Just a few were large – one was 20 feet square and clearly it held a display area for commodities unknown. Later buildings may have encroached on the north and eastern sides of the market place considerably reducing its size – a process known as 'prepresture'. This idea assumes that the original market place was much larger than it is now (about the same size as the present churchyard, of 0.6 acres) and rectangular in shape. If the market place was meant to be 'by-passed' by Red Lion Street, then this might not have been the case. Within the market square there was a market cross and a Toll-House for collecting market or other manorial dues. These would have made the market-square very small unless those buildings were on the site of the present Town Hall.

18. <u>St Michael the Archangel and All Saints Parish Church</u>.

The present church does not sit centrally to the churchyard. This is probably because on the northern side the ground slopes away to the north and the church is aligned with the east end of School Lane. It sits comfortably at the top of the slope. The church is on an east-west axis that is true to the cardinal points yet that axis does not conform with the geometry of the churchyard. This suggests that the original Anglo-Saxon Church could have been placed on a slightly different axis which was corrected when the church was rebuilt in the late 13th century. That is what happened with North Walsham parish church.

Dr Sapwell gives the overall size of the church nave as 164'-9" (50m) by 111'-6"(34m); the chancel length as 53'-3" (16.23m); and the transepts 88'-8" wide (27m). The chancel is described as tall and spacious. Some of the things that have disappeared with time are the Geneva ('Breeches') Bible donated in 1905; a Medieval poor box on a column; the ornamental font cover; several of the late Medieval brasses etc. Dr Sapwell's book on Aylsham states that the church was 'unaltered and has a well proportioned plan'. Daphne Davy (ALHS journal, vol 7, 229) argues that there were three main building phases;

1. Work in Aylsham seems have started at the eastern end in the late 13th century perhaps c1270. The nave followed with its six bays; north and south aisles and a long chancel were built. Its arcade has alternating round piers (something that went out of fashion in the early Decorated period around 1300) and octagonal piers. As the building work progressed further west;

2. The square western tower and south Porch were added in 1300. The south transept was built in 1320 and the northern transept in 1380. This assumes that the church did not have a transeptual plan from the beginning. The latest part displays a transitional Decorated/ Perpendicular style. The north transept came soon after the Dukedom of Lancaster was recreated for John of Gaunt in 1372.

3. The north and south transepts to the Chancel were added c1500; with a 17thc Vestry and charnel chamber built later. All the flints from the previous church were probably 'recycled' in the new building.

The aisles of the nave continue eastwards into the chancel for another two bays. The south wall of the south aisle has large recessed panels which suggest that a further aisle to the south was also envisaged but never built. The clustered piers in the sanctuary are Perpendicular Gothic in style. The chancel arch is corbelled. In the chancel there is a five seat 'Sedalia' with a plain arch over it and a double piscina with simple round bowls.

There is a more elaborate *piscina* in the south transept with an early 16th century traceried canopy and Tudor rose.

IMAGE (3)

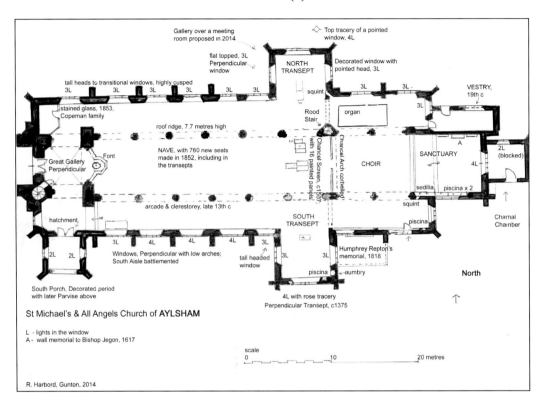

St Michael's & All Angels Church of **AYLSHAM**

L - lights in the window
A - wall memorial to Bishop Jegon, 1617

R. Harbord, Gunton, 2014

1666, the chancel roof was badly leaking so it is surprising the painted panels in the screen below survived without damage. The roof over the nave is a simple frame of principle rafters and intermediaries. It retains some of its Medieval woodwork. All the roofs of the church are leaded. The east window has stained glass of 1842-3. A major restoration of the church took place in 1852 when new pews were inserted to seat 1000 people. For notes on the church bells, see the Appendix.

19. <u>Contents of Aylsham Church and its priests after the Black Death.</u>

The collection of church goods shown in the inventories of 1369 (as listed below) and the wealth of the parish church were extraordinary especially as the former was made at the end of the cycle of plagues called the 'Black Death'. The list enumerates several groups of things which seem to relate to the different side-altars in the church – to St Margaret and St Peter. By grouping the items together we get 6 chalices; 8 sets of vestments with a *tunicle* and *dalmanic*; 13 individual vestments; 18 altar crosses, 2 portable crosses; 18 books etc but there is nothing exceptional in that collection. Someone suggested that the list was so standardised as to suggest that it was not an accurate one but that is conjecture. Many different liturgical books were kept in a parish chest or in some cases, attached to reading desks. This was standard practice at the time. It was only in the 16th century that the different books were combined into a '*Book of Common Prayer*' or a Hymnal.

Printed books did not appear until the mid 16th century so all those in the list were hand written and sometimes richly decorated like 'illuminated manuscripts'. No Bible features in the list – only extracts from the gospels. Church bells were not listed either and again this was fairly usual in Norfolk.

Reference; *Norfolk Record Society*, 1930 pubn vol 19, parts I & 2. Hon Editor, Percy Millican.

CHART (3)

1368, <u>inventory of the church goods in Aylsham.</u>

Books (19) an ordinal	6 surplices
3 antiphones	3 rochets
a prayer book	3 silk cloths
3 psalters	an altar cloth
a manual	2 chalices
a martyrology	2 deaurati
2 missals	18 altar crosses
3 graduals (sung)	a new vestment
2 processionals	a cope
2 sequence books	tunicle & dalmanic
Vestments; 6 pairs of same	a new solempre vestment
2 tunicles	a ordinary? vestment with
2 dalmanics	tunicle & dalmanic
3 copes	an ordinary? silver chalice
Cloths; 6 altar cloths	a new missal
4 hand cloths	vestment, cope, tunicle, dalmanic
3 cloths to cover the sacrament	and hand-cloth
2 more altar cloths	another vestment for chaplain
6 cover cloths for the altar	John de Thurgate
2 altar fronts	vestment for St Peter's altar for same
Articles; 2 silver chalices	vestment for same altar for John Eppe
stone chalice	vestment for the altar of St Margaret
4 cruets	vestment for the altar of St Peter and for
chancel lamp	chaplain Johannen
lantern	a small chest for the Eucharist
censor	a silver Crismatorium
portable cross	silver incense burner
surplice	a restored vestment & silk dalmanic
3 banner staves	an ordinal
2 vestment chests	alb, amita and a velvet stole
a Eucharist pyx	a silk vestment
an oil container	a red cope given by John de Dickleburgh
Incense boat	the vicarage was worth 24 Marks

B. a ruby velvet vestment with blue orphrey at the altar of St Peter for the vicar, Robert de Lenn.
C. silver pectoral (cross), 2 silver cruets, portable silver cross, silver plated chalice.
D. a vestment with gold and ruby; portrait with ornamentation
E. vestment with patches of damask; ex parochial collection. A vestment of John Man, deceased; vestment with black satin patches from diverse parishioners; a gradual, ex collection of John Well & Nicholas Edelinnys; a missal from Robert Man.

<u>Priests mentioned in the inventory list;</u>

<u>Robert Mann</u> - in 1369 he had recently donated a 'new' missal to Aylsham Church. In 1444, a Roger (or, Robert?) Mann recorded the boundaries of the parish. The family had previously owned land in Blickling.

John Well, of Cromer. His Will was proved in 1459. An earlier John Well in Norwich was a wool-merchant; and his wife Margaret was there in Aysham in 1439.

John Eppe, priest, who died in 1377. In his Will he left 2 Marks to the high altar in Aylsham Church; 12d for St Mary's lights; and a cross.

John de Thorney, alias Dickleburgh was the vicar of Aylsham 1349-71, though the clergy list shown below, does not make that clear. He seems to have replaced a previous priest who may have died in the Black Death.

John de Thurgate (-ton?) – Thurgaton is a small parish north of Aylsham.

Nicholas Eddinings.

CHART (4)   Early Priests of Aylsham

Rectors, 1067, Brithric
           gap
           12 . ., John Hastings, presented by Battle Abbey in Sussex.
           1213, William Rowings, presented by King John
               the Crown paid £10 to Battle Abbey for 2/3rds of the great
               tithes.
Vicars, 1225, Rodfrid, presented by Battle Abbey but the Bishop nominated him.
               gap

           1285, Robert
           1299, Eustace of Kimberley
               gap
           1340, John de Lynn
           13…. John de Thorney, alias Dickleburgh
           1372, Thomas Gilman, by Papal nomination.
           13 . . . . John Bromley
           1398, Nicholas Stoke
           1418, Thomas Frengh, of Great Witchingham
           1429, Thomas Booth
           1444, Ralph   Kemp
           1451, Edmund Keche
           1452, Thomas Scrope,
           1484, Henry   Falke
           1489, Christopher Lytton; by Battle Abbey, Bishop nominated
           1490, Thomas Tilson, buried in the chancel
           15… William Bullein
           1542, John Bury, commissary to the Bishop
           1547, Thomas Whitby
           1554, John Bury, LB returned; then he went to Marsham
           1573, Lancelot Thexton
           1581, William Burton; a pluralist
           1584, Moses Fowler, BD
           1591, John Furmarie/ Furmary, by Alice Norgate, widow. He was buried in chancel.
           1610, John Hunt, by the King
           1614, same, by the Dean & Chapter of Canterbury
           1633, John Phillips BD, by Thomas Paston
           1640, Nathaniel Gill
           165…. Edward Bulwer
           1654, Edward Steward
           1657, ... Johnson
           1663, Nathaniel Gill
Reference, C Hugh Bryant's, 'Norfolk Country Churches', 1897? South Erpingham Hundred.

IMAGE (4)
Aylsham parish church from
the south-east.

IMAGE (5)
Interior of the parish
church looking east.

20. <u>Other priests serving the medieval parish church of Aylsham</u>.

The 'de Aylsham' family were closely associated with the early church.
<u>William de Aylsham</u> was rector of Heydon 1361-73, and was buried there. He was a friend of the rector of Cawston.
<u>John de Aylsham</u>, was killed in 1355 in a dispute with Simon de Weston. Edmund Pilcrow tried to intercede in the quarrel and was accused but later acquitted of causing Mr Aylsham's death.
<u>Robert de Aylsham</u> was the vicar of All Saints Church, Lynn. He donated to Aylsham Church a silver Pyx, 2 missals and 2 graduals.
<u>John Flood</u>, vicar of All Saints, Lynn South; 1393 -1404.
<u>John de Brunham</u> was Vicar of Aylsham between 1352-58, though he is not in the official list above. After his stay in Aylsham he moved to Hopton. In 1338, he was in Wood Dalling; then in Walsingham 1338-42; then at the Lazar Hospital in Norwich until 1345; and in Framlingham Earl 1345-53. At some time he also served Hindringham so over a period of about 25 years he occupied seven different Norfolk parishes having survived the Black Death. Is his name confused with John 'Bromley' in the clergy list, whose dates are unknown?
<u>William Gylmyn</u>, chaplain and perhaps brother of Thomas Gylmyn, the vicar of Aylsham, 1371-72.
<u>Thomas Scrope</u>, was the nominal Vicar of Aylsham for 28 years up to 1484. Early in his career he was the Bishop of Dromore in Ireland. He was a Benedictine monk until he

43

arrived in Norwich when he became a Carmelite Friar. He was a man of great learning and wrote several books including one on the rules of the Carmelite Order. He travelled abroad and worked for Pope Eugene IV. He was also favoured by the Knights of Rhodes so he was clearly absent from Aylsham for very long periods. He was buried in Lowestoft.

William Bullein, of Ely and Cambridge University (?) was ordained in 1550 and became rector of Blaxhall, Suffolk. He was ejected by the Puritans and went to London where he practiced medicine. He was accused of killing one of his patients but the courts acquitted him. He died in 1576.

Robert Harrison MA Cantab, was appointed as the master of Aylsham's Free School in 1572. Bishop Parkhurst hesitated to appoint him as Harrison had outspoken views on religion. He was probably asked to keep his opinions to himself but within a month of his arrival in the town he was objecting to the format of the baptism and marriage services in the parish church. The Bishop quickly cancelled his appointment and a Mr Stoon arrived in his place. In the same tense year, plots against the state were unearthed and the Duke of Norfolk was beheaded for treason.

Thomas Furmary, who died in 1610. His widow was murdered in 1622. See later notes on Brasses.

Perhaps the greatest treasure in the church is the magnificent chancel screen.

(Notes taken from the Church Guide Book)

The screen has a series of late medieval panels painted with the figures of the apostles, the evangelists, prophets and patrons. There are various versions in print naming the subjects of the panels. Several of them are easily identified because they hold a personal emblem such as Saint Andrew with his cross. One of the patrons listed below can be identified as his name survives in the script below his image. Other subjects are more obscure as their image has been partly or even entirely destroyed. For further notes see the Appendix on the church.

A Flemish artist seems to have painted on paper the figure in panel 10 and perhaps others (1 and 2?). Part of the screen was once incorporated in the *reredos* behind the high altar, in the 1800s but the present Victorian reredos seem to have disposed of most of it.

1460, a bequest from John Jannys paid for panel no 8 and others.

1507, another from Thomas Wymer and his wives Joan and Agnes paid for some of the painted panels. All this survived the predations of the reformers in the early 1500s but not entirely without damage. Two panels were almost obliterated.

21. Aylsham in the early Middle Ages – an expansion of the population and its farmland.

The Normans provided security and social stability so the economy of north-east Norfolk began to thrive. There were very few permanent desertions of villages in that area. The population of north-east Norfolk began to increase but there is no way of knowing how much of this growth occurred in Aylsham. There were a number of setbacks such as poor harvests, harsh winters, floods and droughts etc. When livestock died in large numbers from disease then there was always the produce of the sea to fall back on for sustenance. By the later 1200s there was a general need for more land to be brought into cultivation. Competing with that was the desire to expand the fold-courses for sheep and pigs in the Severals made from the wild heaths that surrounded Aylsham. This led to (by estimation) about 150 acres of cultivated land being added to the North Field; 350 acres in the West Field and a much smaller area in the East Field – a total of about 500 acres. This was an increase of 25%. It was facilitated by a new invention – the Wind Mill. The two windmills of Aylsham dates from the 19th century but there were probably several post-mills in the parish at a much earlier date. The introduction of this new form of technology meant that cultivated land did not need to be so close to the three water-mills in the parish. That allowed the arable land to be expanded in a northern and western direction.

The new arable land in Aylsham was much smaller in proportion than that converted from heath-land in North Walsham where farmland doubled. There the manorialisation intensified and by 1316 there were eight different manors, each of the recent ones being small, independent and funding their own expansion programme. In Aylsham the story was different. Only two principle Aylsham manors were listed in 1316. These were;

The <u>Manor of the King</u> which he granted (strangely) to a Scottish nobleman – the Earl of Athol. This was Sir David, son of John Strathbogie, by the daughter of the Earl of Mar. He was taken to England in 1300 as a prisoner. On his return to Scotland in 1307 he rebelled against Robert the Bruce in Scotland and had to flee south back into England. In 1316 the English king granted him three Norfolk manors including Aylsham though it is doubtful whether he ever visited them. He commanded the English Army in France during part of the Hundred Years War. In 1322 the Earl was called to the English parliament. 1325 he commanded English troops in France but died in 1326. He was buried in Newcastle-on-Tyne.

The Duchy of Lancaster took over the manor much later – in 1372. Until then the Crown delegated the running of the royal Aylsham manor to local land magnates. After 1372, the Duchy became semi-independent of the Crown Estates and operated in its own way.

The 1316 list of manors in Aylsham left out the smaller estates. These were;
(Reference, '*Feudal Aids*' Norfolk Archaeology vol., 30, p235). The smaller manors were;
1. Battle Abbey Manor. After the dissolution, Aylsham Vicars Manor, was made up mainly of a small collection of church glebe land – too small to be listed.
2. Bolwick Manor, which was only semi-independent of the capital manor of the King from circa 1200 onwards.

One of the places on the west side of the parish is called the 'Warren' but the medieval rabbit warren in the same area seems to have been located just west of the border and in Cawston Parish. No evidence has been found for one in Aylsham.

22. <u>Civil defence arrangements in north-east Norfolk.</u>

The 6th century record of the '*Litus Saxonicum*'; the 'Saxon Shore' listed only the major defences on the Norfolk coast such as the old and then ruined Roman forts such as Burgh-by-Lowestoft. No shore defences were listed for north-east Norfolk but undoubtedly they existed in some form. Happisburgh lies almost mid-way between the Roman stations of Caister-on-Sea to the east and *Branudonum* (Brancaster) to the west. Happisburgh was probably omitted because it had only a landing beach rather than a harbour. There was a relay of signalling stations all along the north coast of Norfolk especially at the high points but no formal list from antiquity has survived. These in turn were connected to key rallying places inland. In fact the whole landscape of north-east Norfolk was partly organised around defence from the earliest times. Possible estate centres like Aylsham would have played a part in that system.

From the Mid Anglo-Saxon period onwards the strongest administrative unit in north-east Norfolk was the one focussed on the Abbey of St Benet's at Horning. Their office was in North Walsham so the mitred abbots (they had a seat in the House of Lords and temporal powers equal to a bishop) of that monastery also acted as 'admirals' of the coast. After the Norman invasion, the responsibility for local defence was taken from the abbots and given to the great magnates who by proxy acted as local war-lords.

Apart from the Roman ditch found on the side of Red Lion Street, there is no other evidence that Aylsham was ever a defended settlement. There were several defended places along the corridor of the River Bure, approaching Aylsham. These included a Roman fort guarding the river-crossing at Horstead; a small moated and crenellated castle at Great Hautbois near the early Norman church (now ruined); and a moated manor-house at Burgh-by-Aylsham. When the Abbots of Bury St Edmunds took possession of the northern part of Aylsham parish, their manor-house was placed near the river and also given a moat. The river itself acted as a defence line along the eastern side of Aylsham.

In the Anglo-Saxon period, the landscape around Aylsham was moulded around food production, hunting (free warren) and civil defence. This meant that the corridors of the River Bure and its tributary streams had a rich habitat for wildlife. The right of warren was the closely guarded preserve of the manorial lords. These corridors were only slowly converted into managed meadows and alder-carr. The Great Wood on the western side of the parish was an area where potentially the population could retreat into; hide and ambush an unwary enemy. By the Middle Ages the residual woods were managed and cropped for timber (see the Appendix) . It is noticeable that after the Conquest the area of woodland in Aylsham was reduced by a quarter. This probably was the result of a steep upsurge in demand for building timber when much of the city of Norwich was rebuilt and expanded by the Normans.

IMAGE (6)

The 'Buttlands', in Aylsham - a medieval archery ground.
From 'Aylsham remebered, 1894-1994', Aylsham Town Council publication, 1995.

There are no grand castles near to Aylsham. Gimingham was a royal *soke* given by William I, to his son-in-law, William Warren. It lies north-east of Aylsham near the coast. It became the new focus of Norman defence of the coast though it was never fortified. Edward I and Edward III made many visits to Norfolk recruiting local men to fight in the French Wars. Especially valued were the Norfolk archers. On the south side of Aylsham town centre are the 'Buttlands' where archery was practiced. It is a narrow strip of land pointing north towards the church tower. It is currently 170 yards long but originally it complied with the statutory length of 220 yards. It stretched from Pinfold Street south to Mill Road where there was a turved embankment behind the target. There is a 'Butts Common' on the northern side of the parish so there there may have been another archery practice area. Archery using the long-bow was the only Sunday sport allowed by law. 'Buttlands' is now the central public car park serving the town centre.

MAP (19)   Defensive sites around Aylsham.

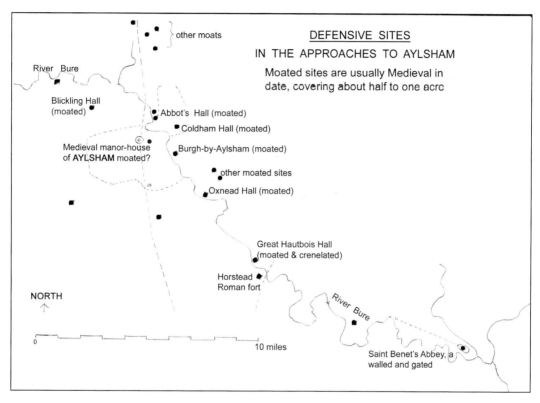

Edward's army sailed from Great Yarmouth to Flanders. Undoubtedly these kings passed through Aylsham before moving on to their local base which was further north in Gimingham. They also stayed there with the Earls of Surrey when they came on pilgrimage to see the holy relics in the great Benedictine monasteries of St Benet's and after 1250, to Bromholm on the coast in Bacton parish (Clunaic after 1195). Henry II was a frequent visitor. Several great magnates also came to north-east Norfolk by sea, landing on local beaches. That reminded everyone how realistic the possibility of an invasion was. Numerous military families like the 'de Erpinghams' participated over several generations in these military campaigns overseas. Sir Thomas de Erpingham at the end of his career came into possession of Blickling Hall and managed the Aylsham Lancaster Manor. These Norfolk knights were celebrated with military effigies and sepulchre brasses in local churches. If memorials were erected to them in Aylsham Church those effigies disappeared when the church was rebuilt in the 14th century. The 'knights fee' attached to each Norfolk manor is a reminder that the local militia had to share garrison duty in Norwich Castle so the local 'muster' of voluntary soldiers was a frequent event.

23. Ecclesiastical jurisdictions.

During the early Anglo-Saxon period, the church's diocese covered all of Norfolk and Suffolk. The centre of the ecclesiastical see was located on the Suffolk coast at *Dumoc* (Dunwich?). That town was near to the secular seat of power, which was focussed nine miles to the south-east at Snape and Rendlesham. The see then moved inland and divided between two places – to North Elmham in the middle of Norfolk; and to South Elmham on the River Waveney in Suffolk.

MAP (20)

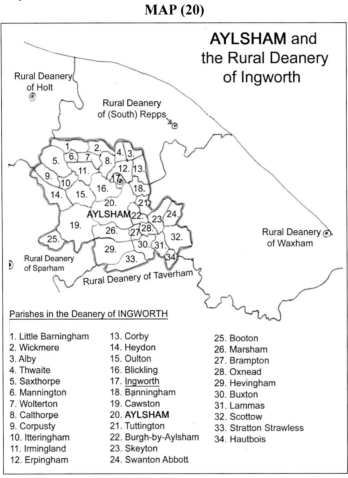

Parishes in the Deanery of INGWORTH

1. Little Barningham	13. Corby	25. Booton
2. Wickmere	14. Heydon	26. Marsham
3. Alby	15. Oulton	27. Brampton
4. Thwaite	16. Blickling	28. Oxnead
5. Saxthorpe	17. Ingworth	29. Hevingham
6. Mannington	18. Banningham	30. Buxton
7. Wolterton	19. Cawston	31. Lammas
8. Calthorpe	20. **AYLSHAM**	32. Scottow
9. Corpusty	21. Tuttington	33. Stratton Strawless
10. Itteringham	22. Burgh-by-Aylsham	34. Hautbois
11. Irmingland	23. Skeyton	
12. Erpingham	24. Swanton Abbott	

Aylsham Church was not mentioned in the Great Survey of 1086. This may have been the consequence of persecution and destruction by the invading Vikings. When the Normans arrived in Norfolk, the centre of the diocese shifted to Thetford for a short time and finally to Norwich. There were no separate Church Deaneries until the Normans created them along with parishes, about 1120. There were about 800 parishes in Norfolk by 1300 but these were reduced to 695 by the mid 18th century. The 120 parishes in north-eastern Norfolk equalled 17% of the total in the county. All the churches of Norfolk were in one arch-deaconry with its ecclesiastical court in Norwich. Then it split into two parts retaining half for itself and a new one was created; the so-called the 'Norwich Archdeaconry'. Aylsham was placed in the latter. The deanery churches were moved away from the market towns which had previously been the hub of church activity and to a village with the oldest know church – in the case of Aylsham it moved to Ingworth.

Ingworth is a tiny parish church and not at all what one would have expected from a deanery church capable of accommodating a large gathering. It has no aisles and the round tower at its western end collapsed in the late 1700s. It has never been rebuilt. Only its tiny nave was slightly widened southwards in the Middle Ages. Much of the Norman fabric survives especially on the northern and western walls of the church. In modern times the residual part of the fallen tower was capped with thatch and converted into a vestry. Besides Aylsham there is another monumental parish church nearby at Cawston but both of them post-date the development of the new Ecclesiastical jurisdictions. Many deanery boundaries follow closely the Hundred boundaries and to a limited extent this applies to Ingworth Deanery. There were many changes to rural deanery boundaries over the centuries though this had little direct effect on Aylsham.

The jurisdictions of the bishop's and archdeacons courts provided an over-sight of church repairs, probate settlements and moral judgements. The Norwich Archdeaconry covered the richest parts of the county. The rural deaneries were abolished in the Reformation but they were revived in 1842.

Ingworth Church is on the old road leading from Cromer to Aylsham and in that way its raised status did not diminish the importance of the latter's parish church. By this date in the early 12th century nearly all settlements had a priest or some kind so Aylsham no longer acted as the hub church or local minster. Yet from early in the Middle Ages church guilds developed. Larger churches like Aylsham contained several guilds. These were essentially lay institutions but they required chantry priests to serve the various altars and images so in that sense they remained 'collegiate'.

The map above also shows the medieval parishes around Aylsham but there is not much of a sign of a radiating pattern of boundaries as seen in say North Walsham. 'Areas of Jurisdiction' were only superseded by the parish system in the Normans period.

24. Weaving in Aylsham and the immigration of skilled workers.

The massive scale of operations needed to hold the sea back and drain the Netherlands defeated them so the first wave of Dutch immigrants came from what is now Holland in the late 1200s.

1290, there was an especially big storm surge that also damaged the coast of Norfolk. Following the Dutch, were the Flemish weavers who travelled from what is now Belgium to settle in Norfolk. Textile production in Aylsham was first recorded about 1300.

1327, Philippa of Hainault married Edward III. Part of the arrangement seems to have been to allow Flemish weavers to emigrate to England, and especially eastern England. When they first arrived in the market towns of north Norfolk like Aylsham, Cawston, North Walsham and Worstead there was hostility from the local population. The courts had to uphold the weavers' claim to carry out their trade freely and without undue impositions. The immigrants soon brought prosperity to these towns. That encouraged the communities to rebuild their churches on a grand scale. Flax for Aylsham linen probably came from the Waveney valley where it was grown in large quantities. There was a continuous traffic of horse-drawn carts carrying raw materials north to Aylsham and the finished products back south again. Some passing references to this subject;

(Ref; *'Norfolk Archaeology'* vol 12, p62; Peter Flint).

1301, the Chamberlayne of Norwich Corporation, made presents of '*Panni de* Aylsham'. Aylsham linen was highly prized.

1315, a complaint was made in Parliament that weavers in Aylsham and Worstead did not observe the standard cloth lengths set out in the Assizes. A 20 measure item was being sold at 24 (d?); a 25 measure at 30 and so on. Aylsham cloth was often bracketed in the accounts with '*buckram*'. This is a stiff cloth usually made from cotton and used for stiffening the bindings of books.

1323; Aylsham cloth was used to make Edward II's pillows and bed linen. A more common use was probably in the provision of burial shrouds known as 'winding sheets' for which there was a large demand.

1327; 3,500 eels of 'Aylsham' were used in the coronation of Edward III – no less that 2½ miles of cloth! It was also bought by the Royal Household to wear under armour; for use as cushions and or the making of 1800 pennants with the cross of St George for a major event. Today this was would have warranted the award of a much coveted badge saying 'by royal appointment'.

1332 Richard Elsing paid 7s-0d for Aylsham linen. By then the town seems to have been the centre of the finishing trade producing sophisticated napery (table linen) spun from flax and course linen derived from hemp.

1333; Aylsham cloth was bought at Christmas for the King's jousting tournament.

1345; by then a *ulnager* (quality controller) was appointed but there was such a big variety of products that he had a difficult job. Also there was strong competition from fine cloth imported from Flanders. While John of Gaunt, or 'Ghent' as was his real title, was living, patronage of Aylsham cloth was supported by the Crown. John was the 4th son of Edward III, born in 1340. In 1359 he married his cousin, Blanche daughter of the 2nd Duke of Lancaster and through her he inherited that title. 'Aylshams' (linen goods) were gradually displaced by worsteds (woollen goods) but their production survived long enough for the 'New Fabrics' or, 'Norwich Stuffs' to take over in the 16th century.

The prosperity enjoyed in Aylsham and North Walsham from weaving was not shared by the surrounding townships. Many weavers found it more profitable to become merchants and move to Norwich in the 1400s. Between 1270 and 1360, 500 Norfolk men mainly from the South Erpingham Hundred moved to London and became mercers. By 1500, linen weaving had long been replaced by wool in Aylsham. Knitted clothes took many forms – gloves, socks, pullovers etc. Cottage industries were a key feature of Aylsham but there is little historic evidence for it now in the surviving old buildings of the town. Many of the weavers occupied the numerous yards and 'lokes' opening off the main streets and especially off Red Lion Street and Hungate.

<u>Other trades and crafts carried out in the town in the 19thc</u>;

The golden age of town based crafts was in the early to mid 1800s. These in Aylsham included; the book keeper, book binder, book seller and stationer; millwright, coach builder, stone mason, artist, clog & pattern maker, clock maker, tea dealer, brazier, cattle dealer, fish monger, net maker, basket weaving; under-takers, dress making, straw bonnets; brewing beer; baking; coffin maker and many others. Part of the stimulus for the growth of these trades was the distance to Norwich; the difficulties and time needed to get there especially when bad weather closed in. Especially during the winter, Aylsham felt cut off from the essential supply of food and fuel. The very large number of shops and stalls recorded in the 1622 Aylsham Lancaster Manor survey show the intensity of market activity in the town. This was a time when there were very few people of independent means of support. From the earliest times Aylsham seems to have made itself self-sufficient in many ways.

25. The Black Death and a fall in population.

During the Middle Ages, small villages like Wolterton; the eastern part of Heveningham and the northern part of Tuttington were abandoned. Only the first two were later resettled. These abandonments may have been because of recurrent plagues throughout the early part of the district's history. A much worse one arrived in 1349 which was repeated to a lesser degree in the summers of 1369, 1375 and 1391. Bateman's list of church institutions suggest that John de Lenn (named after a Norfolk town called Bishop's and then, Kings 'Lynn') was the Vicar of Aylsham between 1340 and 1349. He probably then died in the plague. His replacement, John de Thorney, alias Dickleburgh thrived for many years (see the clergy list above). This and other epidemics often travelled in goods carried between city and town; especially in cloth.

CHART (5)

Taxation reduction after the Black Death			
	__1334__	__1444__	change
Aylsham	£13 10s 0d	£11 10s 0d	-15%
Blickling	£4 10s 0d	same	
Oulton	£4 10s 0d	£2 15s 0d	-39%
Ingworth	£1 6s 0d	same	
Cawston	£12 0s 10d	£10 0s 0d	-22%
Irmingham	£3 12s 0d	£1 12s 0d	-55%
Hautbois Parva	£1	same	
Tuttington	£3 0s 0d	£2 10s 0d	-17%
Burgh	£2 12s 0d	£2 0s 0d	-24%
Oxnead	£1 8s 0d	same	

39 places are listed for South Erpingham Hundred. The total assessments was;
        £132 17s 0d   £ 109 7s 4d   -21%

References.
1. The register of William Bateman, Bishop of Norwich 1344-55, 2 vols; Canterbury & York Society 1996-2000, P E Pobst, editor.
2. '*Norfolk Archaeology*', vol 17, 46-157; the assessment of the townships of Norfolk for the King's 10th and 15[th]s.
3. '*Norfolk Archaeology*', vol 12, p 284-285

The 'pestilence' resulted in a contraction of Aylsham's population size and the amount of agricultural land attached to the town. The only available guides to the size of Aylsham's population are the tax Subsidy lists of **1327, 1332** and **1334** which only gives a small number of tax payers on land and goods. The manorial court rolls might have given extra information but those of Aylsham were destroyed in 1381. Had they survived they would probably show many tenancies without an occupant as there was no-one left to inherit them. The age of a priest that could be installed in a benefice was reduced by Papal authorisation from 24 to 21 years. Norwich was the worst hit place in the county loosing nearly half its population. Rural parishes were hit from 15 - 40%.

The reduction or mitigation of the tax assessment for each parish indicates the amount of population lost. From the figures in the panel above we see that Aylsham came off lightly with a loss of only 15% compared with 21% loss for the whole Hundred. Do these figures reflect the entire picture? It may have been that Aylsham being a prosperous market town was not entitled to such a generous reduction as the less well off rural parishes such as Oulton, Irmingland and Haveringland which remained sparsely populated from then on. In 1428 these had less than ten households in each of their parishes. Although we should treat this figure of 15% with some caution it is the only guide we have of what happened in Aylsham during the Black Death.

The consequences of this drop in population and fall in man-power meant that there was an increasing pressure on agricultural production. With the arrival of the weavers and the increase in independent craftsmen, the number of people employed in farm-work dropped. By 1400, much less than half the population of North Walsham were engaged in farming and the same probably applied to Aylsham. This reduction happened at the same time that the area covered by farming was expanding into the heaths and moors. Non-farm workers resented being pulled into agriculture by a feudal system that required service to the manor right into the 16th century. This resentment was to boil over in the rebellion of 1381.

Enclosure of parts of the common fields accelerated in Aylsham much faster than in neighbouring parishes. This made farming more efficient and less dependent on intensive manual cultivation. Engrossment and consolidation of land holdings also increased after 1400. The 1428 Parish Tax gives some idea of the rapid rate of recovery in Aylsham – but not in many of its neighbours. All this was to come too late to avoid the catastrophe impending at the end of the 14th century.

26. The Peoples Revolution, misnamed the 'Peasants' Revolt'.

Aylsham had acquired a mixed economy by 1381, but the manorial system had not yet caught up with this huge change. In that summer, north-east Norfolk became one of England's epi-centres of rebellion. The Littester brothers were dyers, engaged in work related to the textile industry so they had cause to resent the dysfunctional system of feudalism. They claimed it unjustly enslaved people. Their targets were the centres of big estates like the Lancaster Manor in Aylsham. Liberation meant destroying manorial documents that listed its dependents, their status in the social hierarchy and manorial obligations. By burning these documents it was hoped thereby to free people from manorial servitude. The aim was a spontaneous rising across the whole of England. If that did happen then it would mean that central government could not counter-attack in many places at the same time. Initially that was the measured and reasonable case put forward by the Littesters but it was quickly distracted from events developing in Kent and the assassination of Watt Tyler on the outskirts of London.

From earlier notes we have seen a dozen petty impositions placed on every form of economic and social activity. Then there were the great and small tithes paid to the church and also called the 'tenths' (a 1/10th of income). The accumulation of all of these drove many people to the verge of poverty and beyond. The 'Statute of Labour' held down wages especially for farm workers. On top of that, the Poll Tax added yet another financial imposition to the many fees people had to pay. Some suspected that Richard II was jealous of the wealth and power of his nephew the Duke of Lancaster and so he acquiesced to these additional impositions in order to provoke a rebellion.

The mild request for manorial rolls and charters from local bailiffs soon turned to violence. Thetford was threatened with destruction. When many of the buildings in towns including those of Aylsham were still built principally with timber frames and thatched roofs, destruction by fire was a constant threat. With the receding availability of building timber the prospect of a quick rebuilding programme was also a slender hope. The initial declaration of rebellion was soon followed by petty theft and plunder. It was only after the death of the leader of the Kent rebels, Watt Tyler at Mile End in London on the 15th June that the rebellion in Norfolk began to fall apart. Bishop Despencer of Norwich, an experienced soldier raced from Stamford southwards towards Norwich gathering support from the gentry as he advanced. His quick, decisive but unauthorised action encouraged the rebels to retreat from Norwich northwards to North Walsham. It was on the southern border of that parish, while trying to hold the Bishop's advance up the Norwich Road that the assembled rebels were quickly over-come. Those who escaped retreated to the upper market square and the parish church, barring the entrances but it was to no avail. By the 25th June it was all over. In the subsequent trials of the rebels, several people were identified from the area in and around Aylsham.

(Reference, '*Presentments of Hundred juries established under a commission headed by William de Ufford, Earl of Suffolk, June – July 1381*', National Archives KB9. 166/ 1)

Feudalism in Norfolk defied reform despite Acts of Parliament to that effect in the times of Elizabeth I, and Oliver Cromwell. It even lingered on into the late 19th century when manorial courts were still held in the Black Boys Hotel in Aylsham. By then they were muted affairs and a good chance for socialising around a booze-up yet tenants of the Gunton estate still had to acknowledge and submit to the head of that estate, the 5th Lord Suffield. One reason for the survival of feudalism was that many had common rights which they did not wish to give up or were unable to collectively purchase. Some of those rights even survive to this day especially where nearly a whole village or parish remains in a single ownership. There are several examples of that around Alysham. Feudalism has indeed never completely disappeared because it is bound up inextricably in property law.

During the 15th century wool production gained greater economic importance. To some extent Aylsham Parish Church is a 'wool church' as many of its richer features benefitted from the wool trade. Aylsham parish did not have extensive sheep fold-courses as we would have seen in western Norfolk for example. The south-western part of the parish south of the Great Wood and along Stonegate was the scene of the largest areas of pasture. Whether this had previously been cultivated and then reclaimed for sheep is not known. The large belt of moors alluded to above on the west side of the parish and stretching down to Norwich was the area most suitable for sheep grazing. Norfolk sheep then were very different from the large woolly cross-bred sheep we see today. They were lean; had black faces, long legs and were much better suited to living outdoors in all weather conditions. After harvest time, pasture extended over most of the parish.

27. <u>The Protestant Reformation and its effect on Aylsham</u>.

By the late 15th century the Reformation was in full swing and it was supported by many of the catholic clergy. This trend was opposed by the official Roman Catholic Church who promoted a 'Counter Reformation'. The expression of that cultural movement meant that church interiors were festooned with gaudy decorations such as mural paintings and scrolled texts; painted panels in chancel screens; images carved in wood or stone; candles etc etc.

There were many bequests to the parish church of Aylsham in the late Middle Ages. Most of the bequests that have come down to us through the records were made in the late 1400s and early 1500s. They were usually given for a specific purpose. The completion of

Aylsham's parish church seems to have come soon after John of Gaunt's acquisition of the Dukedom of Lancaster in 1372. Did he attend with the bishop the rededication of the new church? His coat-of-arms can be seen on the south Porch. Although that great magnate may have patronised the project, it is likely that the bulk of the finance came from the ordinary folk of the town.

Church Guilds had been around for at least a century but by 1400 they gained momentum and support. Only a few, local and medieval guild-lists have survived like the one from Suffield. It shows that almost every resident in that parish was a guild member. It was sort of mutual benefit society or form of insurance that replaced the declining support provided by the defunct feudal system. Guilds had elected officers who were independent of the clergy, such as a treasurer. They had their own premises for feastings on the saint's day. This celebration followed a procession and service of thanks-giving in the church. After paying their modest subscription everyone in the parish joined in and no wonder – it was a great source of local jolly making. The 1369 church goods list of Aylsham Church (see above) includes staves to hold up banners decorated with the emblems of a particular guild. The Guilds of St Peter and St Margaret were mentioned in Aylsham Church each with its chapel, altar, image etc. **MAP (21)**

Many of those who left bequests were allowed to be buried inside the church with their own family ledger slabs, indented to take a memorial brass. Five of them survive in the church but the list provided in the Appendix shows there were once many more. Special masses and ringing of the bells were made in their perpetual memory and that increasingly underlined social divisions in the community. This caused resentment which found expression in a resistance to the dogma of the church, including the way it was decorated and laid out. It ultimately led to a wave of destruction by the Puritans in the mid 1500s and the mid 1600s. This was linked to the growing economic and social independence of wealth amongst the land-owning mercantile and professional classes. By the 1500s Aylsham was starting to become 'gentrified'. New and larger

MILLGATE - THE NORTHERN SUBURB OF AYLSHAM

An extract from the 1839 Tithe Survey Map of AYLSHAM (NRO)

houses were being built in the town and on its edges. The poorer people usually occupied smaller dwellings up the lokes, yards and alleys opening off the main streets of the town centre. These were often only one storey high perhaps with a roof space for sleeping in. If they had two rooms, one would have been used for cottage industry to hold a loom or another type of workshop. The living room accommodated all other domestic activities including sleeping. Some of this type of dwelling survived into modern times in the northern extension to the town. The development of Millgate (see the map above) took place mainly in the 19th century but dwellings from an earlier period survived there into the early 20th century.

IMAGES, 7 - 8; Aylsham Parish Church

14th century south porch with a 'parvis' chamber added above later.

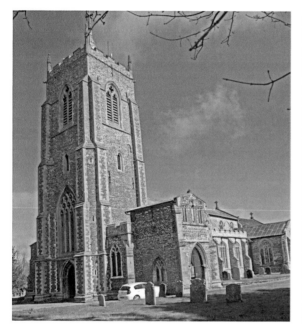

The clearest evidence of prosperity in the early 1500s came with the embellishment of the parish church. These two pictures of the church were taken from the south-east (left) and south (right). One shows the tower with its elaborate lead spire giving it a total height of 100 feet. With very tall towers in adjacent towns – Cromer, Cawston, Southrepps, North Walsham etc it was important to keep up with the neighbours! The rebuilt church was rather plain until battlements were added to the tower parapet and the south aisle (only). This feature became popular in the 15th century. The addition of a '*parvis*' chamber over the south porch added a great deal of quality. A frieze around the porch has panels of flushwork with masonry framing cut flints. In the centre are the Arms of England with a Fleurs-de-Lis and the cross of St George on either side. The central niche, now empty may have originally have had a carved image of the patron saint, St Michael. The tracery and flattened arches of the large south windows compliment the late Perpendicular style of the Porch. The spiral stair to the Parvis Chamber is now blocked – it was used to store ammunition during the Napoleonic Wars (listed in the Appendix). The church was probably re-roofed in lead at this time though there is no surviving evidence of an earlier form of roofing needing a steeper pitch. The inside of the church was also embellished by new features. The tower received new bells and bell frames. In the 1552 sequestration survey of church goods there were five.

55

A square bell-ringers' gallery was added inside the tower space and amazingly it is still there. A pair of great, timber posts stand on each side, carrying a flattened and decorated beam. In the south-western corner is a small door to the spiral stair leading up to the gallery and the higher stages of the tower. Old church guides say it had 'interesting iron work' in the hinges, handle etc but this seems to have been replaced in recent times perhaps for security reasons. Further east is the baptismal Font placed on a podium of three steps. The climax of the late 15th and early 16th century features of the church is the Chancel Screen. The traceried upper section, beam, loft and its parapet and the Rood Cross have all been lost. What survives is the very narrow spiral stair in the north pier of the chancel arch and its upper doorway. Also the lower portion of the screen survives against all the odds.

IMAGES, 9 – 10, from the chancel screen of Aylsham Church.

The images above have been digitally enhanced to remove the scars left by the Puritans. It seems that the northern part of the screen survived almost intact because pew benches were placed against it yet even the images above bare evidence of wilfull damage in the 16th and 17th centuries? Images in some churches were plastered over but then how could these paintings on paper survive such treatment? From a secular point of view it is the two portraits of its patrons on the left hand side of the screen that are of the greatest interest. These were Thomas Wymer shown above right; and John Jannys, above left.

28. Developments in Aylsham in the 16th century.

John and Agnes Jannys were the earlier donors for the chancel screen in the parish church. Their son Robert Jannys (Image 11) left funds in his Will towards the endowment of a free school in Aylsham – the first in the town. This contributed £10 each year towards the school master's salary. The school in a different form still survives today. Jannys was born in Aylsham. He became Sheriff and then Mayor of Norwich in 1517 and 1524. He died in 1530.

<u>Robert Jannys</u>. Ref, '*The art of faith; 3500 years of art & belief in Norfolk*', by A. Moore and M. Thøfner'; a Norwich City Art Gallery pubn 2010. **IMAGE (11)**

The impact of the Reformation was felt in 1537 where several men demanded from the Church Wardens the keys to the parish chest. They feared that the church plate estimated to be worth £500 was about to be sequested by Royal Commissioners. This was an echo of the 'Pilgrim of Grace' which demonstrated in the North of England against the destruction of sacred images. Edmund White, John Jones, John Tolwin and John Baker of Aylsham wanted to sell the plate before it was lost to the town. They threatened to charge the church wardens with the value of the plate if it was lost. In fact it was eventually sold in 1546 and in 1552 the long feared event did happen when Commissioners went around all the parish churches of the diocese taking all but the essential and valuable moveables with them. The inventory of goods removed from Aylsham Church was probably only a small part of what had been there in 1537.

The changes to the landscape of Aylsham in this period can only be guessed at. The rate of conversion of the open fields probably progressed faster than in the adjacent parishes. Enclosure was advancing rapidly by the late 16th century across the district. This can be seen from the 1580 survey of Cawston which is a parish that lies to the west of Aylsham. The map shown below is kept in Cambridge University Library. The three large open fields (shown coloured green) remained. Many of large closes on their boundaries represented *assarts* into the surrounding heath-land. Wood Lane can clearly be seen running north and south through a heath shared with Aylsham and Marsham to the east.

MAP (22)

CAWSTON survey map 1580
Cambridge University archives

The open fields of Cawston were to the west. During the early Middle Ages the extent of the heath probably extended further west of Wood Lane. By 1580 the north (Bayfield) open field had 'recently' been enclosed but still a lot more than half of the parish was an open landscape. There were considerable variations between parishes but Aylsham and Cawston were linked in several ways. The former may have reached a similar stage of enclosure at this date, 1580. Without a comparable survey plan, that has to be speculative.

The map below shows that the densest part of the population of north-east Norfolk was still concentrated in the towns and large villages, leaving huge tracts of the countryside in this very rural part of Norfolk with a low level of population. At this stage in history it also reflects the distribution of wealth – before the big landed estates developed around country houses.   **MAP (23)**

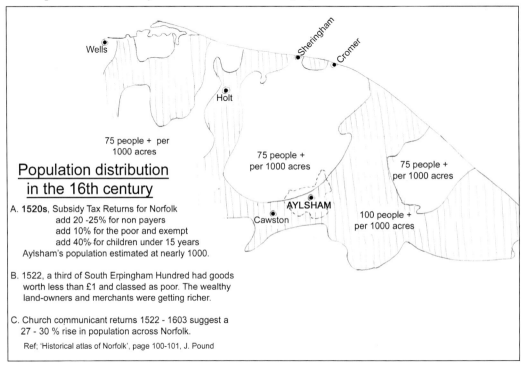

Reference; '*Historical Atlas of Norfolk*', Phillimore pubn, 2005, Trevor Ashwin & Alan Davison, co editors, page 101 by John Pound.

Between 1334 and 1525, there was a decline in taxable wealth in Norfolk but Hevingham was an exception despite having poor soils. The decline occurred where there were strong lordships. Townships like Aylsham also bucked the trend. South Erpingham Hundred saw an actual rise of 18.2 %, or 3% if the urbanised town of Aylsham was excluded.

29. Buildings in Aylsham during the 17th century.

Many towns in Norfolk, such as North Walsham and Holt were destroyed by fires that swept away all those parts of the town that lay in the direction of the wind. Their timber-frames and thatched roofs probably burnt for days. Buildings were usually tightly packed around the burial yard of the parish but that didn't provide much of a fire break in a great conflagration. This sort of catastrophe does not seem to have happened in Aylsham which is why so many early timber-framed houses still survive today. In the 1622 survey the 'Tiled' house in the market place was given a special mention as most other houses and shops were still thatched. Most of the reed thatch came from the Norfolk Broads via the North Walsham market place. Aylsham has always had a number of gentry living in the parish but in 1614 a celebrity moved into the manor-house. This is situated near the junction of the Norwich and Burgh roads. Long brick walls on the side of the main Norwich Road now enclose its extensive grounds. It became the home of John Jegon former Master of Corpus Christi College, Cambridge and later, Bishop of Norwich. To save money he left his cathedral palace in the centre of Norwich and moved to a large house in Ludham. This building had previously burnt down and in 1614 it burnt down again. Bishop Jegon had bought a retirement home in Aylsham – the manor house. His date for moving in was brought forward! He only lived there for four years after which he died. A fitting memorial was erected to him in the chancel of Aylsham Church which is now fully restored. His wife was much younger. She and her children lived on in the area for some time afterwards. Jegon was a noted disciplinarian in regard to church matters though he was more tolerant than later bishops in regard to religious conformity.

IMAGE (12) Blickling Hall

In **1622** Sir John Hobart of Blickling Hall (shown above) was granted a 22 year lease on the freehold of the Aylsham Lancaster estate by James I. Sextons or Woods Manor was absorbed into the capital manor at the same time. Later he bought both from the Crown. At the same time he began to rebuild Blickling Hall on a monumental scale – it is one of the biggest mansions in East Anglia. Today it is the National Trust's Eastern Regional head-quarters. It remains largely intact and unaltered from the time of the same Sir John Hobart. The arrival of the Hobart family and their huge investment in Blickling brought an immense amount of prosperity to Aylsham which became its service town.

The grandest house in Aylsham built in the 17th century was the Old Hall which dates from **1686**. It seems to have been built for the Windham family of Felbrigg Hall (now owned by the National Trust and lying a few miles north of Aylsham). Its building style is very similar to the later part of Felbrigg. Was it intended to be a dower house for Felbrigg? The Old Hall was not bought by the Blickling estate until 1751 when it was occupied by Robert Copeman, the land agent of the 2nd Earl of Buckinghamshire, of

Blickling. See the Copeman family memorials in Aylsham Church. It was originally laid out in the grand manner with a large barn and a formal walled garden on the north side. The only changes to the outside have been a replacement of the high pitched hip roof; and sash windows instead of the original cross-casements. Otherwise Pevsner describes it as 'the perfect specimen of an early classical house'.

IMAGE (13)

Rebuilding the town's buildings with brick walls and clay-tiled roofs followed from this lead. The next big house was the new Vicarage built in 1700. In 1710, the Black Boys Hotel was encased in a classical brick frontage and a shaped northern gable. Many other houses in the town were re-fronted at this time in a similar manner while retaining their much older structure behind the new façade. Aylsham still boasts many Dutch house gables. It is difficult today to appreciate what an advance these developments were but in the early 1700s many of the humbler houses were still one, or one and a half storeys high.

30. <u>Landscape changes in the 17th century.</u>

In **1622** a survey of the Duchy of Lancaster's estate in Aylsham was made at the time when it was mortgaged to the City Corporation of London. There had been in recent years a long wrangle between the Duchy and its Aylsham tenants. The total area of the Duchy's estate amounted to about 2,300 acres, (see the Appendix list of holdings) or nearly half the area of the present parish of Aylsham of 4,300 acres. The survey reveals that almost 600 acres had been recently enclosed by then. Over half (1,244 acres) remained unenclosed in furlongs and strips. The remainder was made up of meadows, pasture and woodland. The overall amount of land being farmed does not represent a huge jump from the figure in the *Domesday Survey* made in 1050-86, namely 2,100 acres.

The Aylsham Vicars Manor was so small in land area that it can be ignored for these calculations. Woods Manor probably covered only 300 acres at the most in 1086, so the net increase in area covered by arable land was small. The total increase in land used for arable farming between 1086 and 1624 was about 500 acres in about 550 years or +25%. A large part of that came from the reduction in size of the Great Wood. The 1622 survey includes small areas such as meadow, pasture, recently converted from woods or heath-land so the increase of arable land was perhaps less than 500 acres.

Settlement often dispersed to the edges of the fields – something that did not happen in Aylsham where there appears to have been firmer control. Many small parcels of land in Aylsham were listed in 1624 – most of them being field strips. Some closes are mentioned but even they were sometimes sub-divided into strips. Most enclosures took place over the following century by which time few of the remaining furlongs were still divided into small strips.

MAP (24)

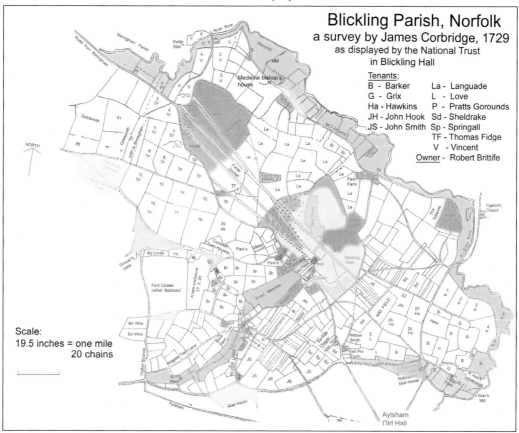

Blickling lies on the northern side of Aylsham and it is worth studying for purposes of comparison. Its Park was (and still is) so large that only a few of the open furlongs remained by the early 1700s. The surviving strips shown on the 1729 survey plan seem to have been re-aligned as the open fields contracted. No clear pattern of furlongs can be interpolated from this plan, unlike the open fields of Aylsham. The great medieval wood and park in the centre of the parish give it a very different shape and pattern to Aylsham so again there is a limit to the comparisons that can be drawn between the two. No enclosure map has been found for Aylsham so it can be assumed that the parish was already enclosed by the early 1700s.

The 17th century saw the appearances of the earliest farmsteads built in or often on the edge of medieval the open fields. This saw the transformation of the open landscape into a patchwork of geometric enclosures lined with ditches, hedges and trees which is the landscape familiar to us today. Field boundaries often followed those of the old Furlongs; their balks, field ways and hedges, which provide us with some idea of what had preceded them. There were two independent estates within the capital manor of the Aylsham Duchy. One was owned by Bishop John Jegon. When he died in 1618 his estate was inherited through the widow, by her second husband, Sir Charles Cornwallis, namely 293 acres. This area may be similar if not identical to the 19th century estate of John Bulwer (shown the Map below, which was focussed on the Aylsham Manor House. It extended into the south-eastern part of the town centre with 18 fields and one strip.

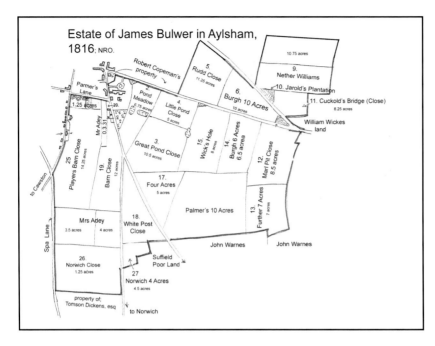

MAP (25)

IMAGES (14) & (15)

John Jegon, 1550 – 1618; Dean and then Bishop of Norwich.

The memorial to Bishop Jegon on the north wall of the chancel of Aylsham Parish Church is emblazoned with his coat of arms topped by a bishop's mitre. At the base is a skull with ribbons. The memorial is made of alabaster marble and designed in a classical format including a pediment. It was once enclosed with a small iron railing .

IMAGE (16) <u>Sir Charles Cornwallis</u>, c1560-1629 (left).

He was born in Brome Hall, Suffolk and became the Controller of Queen Mary's household. Knighted in 1603, he was MP for Norfolk in 1604. He served as the Ambassador to Spain 1605-09 but was imprisoned in the Tower in 1614. It was about 1620 when he married his third wife, Dorothy Vaughan and came briefly to Aylsham. She was the daughter of the Bishop of London and the widow of Bishop John Jegon. Cornwallis was buried in London; his age unknown.

Another gentry family were the Jermys of Bayfield Hall, near Holt. Their large, early 18th century tomb is in the south aisle of the Church (seen below). It shows that landed families from outside the parish retained a material interest in Aylsham in this period. This was partly because gentry widows seem to have retired there. An example of this may have been Rebecca Wrench, sister of the Vicar of Aylsham whose husband Colonel Harbord Cropley Harbord of Gunton Hall died in 1741.

Below, is the memorial to the Jermy family and a cartouche carved with their Arms.

IMAGES (17 – 18) with the cartouche on the side.

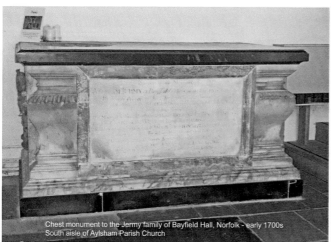

Chest monument to the Jermy family of Bayfield Hall, Norfolk - early 1700s
South aisle of Aylsham Parish Church

This monumental tomb originally stood at the eastern end of the north aisle of the church but in the 1852 refurbishment programme it was moved to its present position at the west end of the south aisle. It was Mrs Jermy of Bayfield who generously left a silver plate to the church though there had been great hope that much more could have been expected from her Will! Nearby and over the south door of the church hangs a Hatchment which is related to this tomb. It includes the Arms of the Jermy family as well as those of Bigod, Mountenay, Yelverton, Cock, Wrench, Fuller, Sturkey,and Weld families.

Another example of a gentry family were the Doughtys of Hanworth Hall whose relatives played a prominent part in the life of Aylsham in the 16th and 17th centuries. Many were church-wardens and there were several Robert Doughtys.

The Bolwick estate was a bit smaller than the Jegon – Bulwer estate at 169 acres – no estate map has been found of its extent. By 1700 there were few woods left and a new movement began to install plantations. A nation-wide impetus was made by the squire whose family originated from the adjoining parish of Marsham – Robert Marsham. The other big change in the landscape was the conversion of former sheep folds to cultivation. This was aided by the development of the yeoman farmer and his farm detached from the main settlement. Some of the farms of Aylsham parish date back to the 17thc.

31. Population changes in the 17th centuries in Aylsham.

A big jump in the size of the Aylsham's population began in the mid 1600s. The 'Collection for poor distressed Irish Protestants' in **1643** (PRO Kew, SP 28/ 294) survives for over half the parishes of Norfolk but the one for Aylsham has not been found. Had it done so then it could have included signatures for most of the adult population of the parish. An almost contemporary list of names of Aylsham people does however survive (the 'Solemn League of the Covenant', signed on 20th January 1643.
(Reference; House of Lord's Library, HL/ PO/ JO/ 10/ 1/ 67 – South Erpingham Hundred).
This has 349 names in it though 75 of them are unreadable. They include;

Robert Doughty (top)	
Rev John Philip, minister	
Thomas Knolls	Robert Betts, church warden
John Neane,	Thomas Harvey, constable
William Doughty	John Ellis, a mark
Dorcas Woods	
Nathaniel Woods, etc	

This list covered just under half of the adult population aged over 14 years assuming that the population was then still around 800.

CHART (6) Extracts from the records of Hearth Tax assessment.

7. Hearth Tax; *Norfolk Genealogy* vol 20; 1666 blank ; vol 15, 1664 –
Total - 132 names; 385 hearths for houses not exempt. 33 were large houses with 4 or more hearths. Extract;

	Rev Lancelot Thexton		5
10 hearths; 1 house	Mr Christopher Taylor		3
	Mrs William Doughty		4
8 hearths; 2 houses	Matthew	Fairchild	2
	Thomas	Knight	8
7 hearths; 1 house	Elizabeth	Lubbock	5
	John	Goole	8
6 hearths; 4 houses	John	Crow	4
	Major (Robert?) Doughty		9
5 hearths; 11 houses	Thomas	Barker	7
	John	Thompson	8
4 hearths 14 houses	Rev Nathaniel	Gill	5
	Edmund	Harrod	2
	Margaret	Anderson	4
	Humphrey	Allison	5

The 1666 Hearth Tax assessment lists 138 house-holders who were payers. Another list giving those who were exempt has not been found. It would have included the vicar, widows and the poor. Many of those people would be housed in single occupancy dwellings. Using an estimated average of 4.5 people per dwelling, gives a population of about 500. If we add say 200 hundred exemptions it is a figure well below the assumed total population of 800 people.

CHART (7)

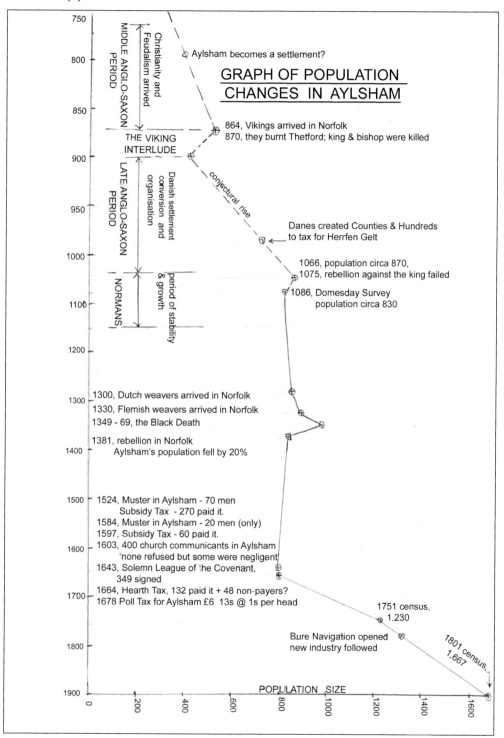

By **1691** the population stood at 810, so if the earlier figure accrate then there was a rise in population during the 17th century. Even if correct that means that the total size of population of Aylsham had not substantially changed overall since the *Domesday* Survey in 1086. This does not discount large fluctuations such as the population rise in the early 14th century and the fall due to the Black Death when an estimated 120 people were lost.

32. Events in Aylsham in the 17th century.

A great legal battle developed in the early 1600s between the Hobart family of Blickling Hall and the tenants of the Aylsham Lancaster Manor and that meant most of the residents of the parish. It is tempting to believe that had Bishop Jegon not died in 1618 he might have acted as an arbiter in this dispute. Sir Henry Hobart (see the portrait below) was the Chancellor to the Prince of Wales and that was to give him an unfair advantage in the contest. He bought the Parsonage tithes, lands and mills in Aylsham as well as the Berewick of all the Lancaster estates in East Anglia. Sir Henry died in 1626 and was succeeded by his son Sir John Hobart (no portrait of him has been found) who seems to have been less confrontational.

IMAGES (19 - 20)

Sir Henry Hobart, 1st Bart of Blickling Hall and his wife Dorothy Bell married in 1590.

When Sir John died in 1647 most of his lesser properties associated with Aylsham had to be sold off to pay his debts and anyway, the Berewick proved not to be a lucrative office.

In 1622 Sir Henry won the first round against the tenants with the award of a 23 year lease on the manor starting in 1630 when the tenants lease ended. The total rents from the manor were only £44-0s-7d per year. Edmund Reeve the steward to the manor court suggested to Sir John that he buy the estate outright. He offered £600 to the City of London Commonality who owned the reversion. One of its members had contacts in Aylsham and they gave the tenants the tip-off. They offered £800 and when Sir John increased his offer, the tenants raised their bid to £1200 – a bid that was accepted. Sir John then petitioned the king to set aside the tenants' claim to 'ancient property rights' and their bid. In view of the king's debt to his father Sir Henry, he duly complied and Sir John acquired the manor. The tenants had to relinquish their bargain of sale. It was an expensive exercise but a far sighted one for Sir John. It preserved the integrity of the parish and stopped the westward spread of the town into the open landscape of Blickling.

The tenants did win a few concessions. The Hobarts were to repair the Market Cross; hold fines to 3s to 4s per acre; tenants were allowed to sell leases for up to 21 years etc. In 1641, the tenants applied for the fine to be reduced to 1s-6d per acre. That time they were successful. Given the long term feud between the Hobarts of Blickling and Aylsham it is surprising that there was no confrontation between them during the Civil War period. In fact the Hobarts were steadfast supporters of the Parliamentary cause during this period which pre-empted any such idea.

In October 21, **1641** local MPs, magistrates and deputy Lord Lieutenants met in Aylsham, presumably at the Black Boys Hotel to pool their liquid assets (ie mainly silver plate and cash) to support Parliament in its struggle against the Crown. The whole of the South Erpingham Hundred was supposed to be united it that support so the only resistance to it seemed to rest mainly with the Anglican clergy.

Many of the clergy in north-east Norfolk were forcibly ejected from their benefices at this time – often for refusing to read out from their pulpits declarations issued to them by Parliamentary agents. An example was the Rev Nathaniel Gill of Burgh-by-Aylsham. He was rector of Burgh from 1638 to 1644. After his ejection he carried on in secrecy serving his parish until 1651 when he was finally removed on the orders of the Earl of Manchester, Parliament's chief authority in Eastern England. Gill returned triumphantly to his parish at the Restoration in 1660 and served there until 1663 when he became Vicar of the much richer benefice of Aylsham. Apart from that interlude he served Burgh for 25 years. Other priests in the district were less lucky and they often endured much hardship. Richard Howes, the rector of Knapton was incarcerated in the unpleasant lock-up of Aylsham where his cell-mates included a dangerous criminal. It was only after his release that Howes was able to protest and have the man removed to the grim dungeons of Norwich Castle gaol.

A mini rebellion saw the civil war coming close to Aylsham when a group of people paraded into the market square. This was in April **1643** when there was a protest against levies rated on the local population to support Parliament's struggle. A posse of trained soldiers rode quickly from Norwich Castle up the Aylsham Road and stormed into the square. Many of those who were arrested were local business men, minor land-owners and lawyers; ie not the poor people who had rebelled in 1381. Bishop Jegon's son Robert had gone to live in Buxton and he came under scrutiny from the authorities for supporting this demonstration. Demonstrators who were arrested and charged had to attend a hearing in front of a sequestration committee held in the Goldsmiths Hall, in the City of London. Draconian fines were imposed on the demonstrators. They had to pay a third to a tenth of their estates which could amount to as much as £1000. This shows how rich these land-owners had become over the previous century.

The later part of the 17th century saw the social rise of the Doughty family. They had been established in the Metton area since the 1400s and by the 1500s they owned the modest manor-house of Hanworth. They travelled over-seas to the burgeoning empire and on their return they began to buy up land in north-east Norfolk. The brothers Doughty became church-wardens in Aylsham by 1677 but they soon got into a legal conflict with the vicar. This saw others rise in social status to minor gentry such as the Norgate family. Three Norgates feature in the 1597 tax subsidy list for Aylsham. Several of them studied in Cambridge University and often the males of the family became priests. By 1614, Henry Norgate was the steward of the Aylsham Lancaster Manor.

The earliest church terrier dates from 1677 and it notes the small amount of glebe land owned by the church – only 5 acres. This was partly because so much of the church's property had been sold off in the mid 1500s to avoid its wealth being sequested by the Crown. The Rev Robert Fawcett was vicar of Aylsham between, 1669 and 1687. When he died in 1699 an inventory was made of his estate. It was worth the substantial sum of £224-14s-6d. This inventory describes the Vicarage before it was rebuilt by the later vicar, Jonathan Wrench in 1700. The earlier house had a dining hall, a great parlour, a little parlour – perhaps the study, four bedrooms and the usual domestic offices. The stables were occupied by cows and pigs as well as two horses. (NRO; NCC 688/ 23). Numerous Wills were proved in the Norwich Courts and there are seven probate inventories for Aylsham made in the 17th century. Given the wealth in Aylsham, few Wills were proved in the Court of Canterbury except for the mid 17th century when perhaps there was a mistrust of the Ecclesiastical Courts in Norfolk, or were they just inactive?

33. Aylsham in the 18th century.

CHART (8)

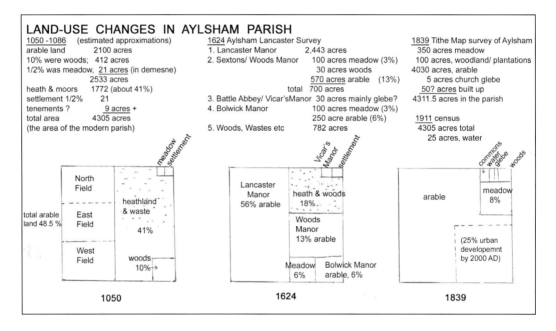

This was the century when the last vestiges of feudalism were swept away - almost. The majority of the common fields had been enclosed by the late 1700s. Tenants from the large neighbouring estates continued to pay homage to the lords of the manor right into the late 1800s. They attended the Black Boys Hotel, swore fealty to the manor and promised to be law-abiding. They were then allowed to hold onto their tenancies (and homes!) and offered a free drink in the bar below. The Gunton Estate contained 15,000 acres so it meant that Lord Suffield had an 'army' of tenants. The Blickling estate was much smaller until the 2nd Lord Suffield married the heiress of the 2nd and last Earl of Buckinghamshire in Blickling in 1792. About 2,000 acres was transferred from the Gunton estate to Blickling bringing it up to its present extent of nearly 5,000 acres. This is not large in proportion to the scale and magnificence of Blickling Hall especially when nearly 1000 acres is made up of parkland and woods. William Harbord and Caroline Hobart were second cousins who shared the same great grand-father Robert Britiffe, the

Norwich MP. Britiffe accumulated very large amounts of property which were shared out between the two families including land in Blickling. The latter returned to the Blickling estate and the manorial rights to Aylsham though not much land came with it.

These big estates and the smaller ones like those attached to Bolwick Hall and Aylsham Manor House helped to rationalise the landscape into a grid of fields enclosed with hedges, ditches and trees. Romantic landscape artists of the Norwich school celebrated in their pictures the informality of the previous age as it drifted away. By the end of the century there were farms at Woodgate, Sankence, Meadow Hill, Spa, Diggens, Stapltons, Spratts Green, Bolwick Hall, Bure Valley, Valley (Manor), Abbot's, Hall Ash Tree, Church, Coldham Hall as well as other small–holdings. The holdings of these fourteen larger farms are listed with their occupants in the 1839 Tithe Map, by which time the reconfiguration of the landscape was complete (see Maps in the Appendix).

This was brought to a conclusion during the Napoleonic Wars when the need for greater agricultural production was intensified. Humphrey Repton was one of the local leaders in this process. He is better known as someone who placed power and privilege in the landscape through his designs of country parks and gardens on a national scale but in the late 1790s he was a member of a specialist team based at Felbrigg a few miles north of Aylsham bringing the Agricultural Revolution to north-east Norfolk. His direct impact on Aylsham is unknown but his brother farmed nearby at Oxnead.

IMAGE (21) Attached to Aylsham Church is his family's memorial (see left) and there is also a stained glass window inside, dedicated to him. Humphrey often stayed in Aylsham with his sister Dorothy, Mrs Adey. In 1800 and later he was advising on the layout of the grand gardens and decorative features in the park of Blickling. Perhaps some of his drawings and sketches were made in the family house at no 1, The Market Square. This work was continued by his son John Adey Repton the architect, who also made proposals for works in Gunton Park to the north of Aylsham. Their association with Aylsham and Blickling lasted from c1780 to the late 1820s.

Artists of the Norwich School began to recognise the scenic beauty of Aylsham, or at least parts of it. An early scene of Mill Road area survives. Robert Ladbrooke's drawing of the parish church of the 1820s, is the earliest known view showing it before the Victorian restoration of 1852. It had changed little since 1500. Rev James Bulwer was an artist born in the town who later moved to Hunworth in Norfolk. He made several water coloured pictures of the town in the mid 1800s – one showing the river and bridge; another looking north along Hungate Street.

The hold on religion by the Anglican Church was relaxed in the 1700s. Non-conformists began to build their own meeting houses and chapels in the town. Previously, private houses were used for meetings and the Roman Catholics continued to do so until they were able to eventually establish their own premises in the 1900s. Despite all this social progress, the archaic system of drawing water from wells and disposal of waste-water through cess pits survived well into the 19th century. Systematic water and energy supply had to wait until the mid-20th century. Some wells were very deep – the Town

Pump at the northern end of Cawston Road is reputed to be 180' deep. It was reopened in a public ceremony and provided with an open thatched canopy in 1913.

The early list of voters in the County Poll Books give some idea of the number of wealthier people living in Aylsham and also the number of substantial properties there.

1714; 5 names only were listed including the Vicar, Jonathan Wrench.

1768; 18 names. This is also a very small number of people given that the population of Aylsham had recently risen sharply between 1741-51, from 990 to 1230 people.

1802; 24 names, when the population had again risen dramatically to 1667 according to the census. It had doubled since 1691, just over a century before.

One of the finest new Georgian houses in Aylsham was built in 1760. The West Lodge was built by Lord Townsend of Raynham Hall, Norfolk to accommodate his mistress Elizabeth Walker. It became the grandest house in the parish until Bolwick Hall was extended in the early 1800s. It still has extensive grounds and a walled kitchen garden.

Three storey Georgian town houses faced the south and east sides of the market place including John Adey's house where Humphrey Repton stayed. He was articled to Adey who was one of the town's attorneys. It still has a fine classical framed doorway.

1780, Parson Woodford visited the Black Boys Inn, Aylsham but as usual in his famous diary he focussed mainly on the enormous amount of food he consumed underlining the comfortable well-being amongst the middle classes. There was also a series of calamities in this fragile century;

A plaque on the south-eastern corner of Aylsham's market place records the martyrdom of Christopher 'Kit' Layer in 1723. One of his ancestors was the Mayor of Norwich who bought the manor of Booton. It was there that Kit was born in 1677. Articled to Aylsham attorney, Henry Rippenhall he married a local girl, Elizabeth the daughter of Peter Elwin of Aylsham.

IMAGE (22) Christopher Layer

James Stuart the Old Pretender landed in Scotland in 1715. When the Rising failed, he fled back to the Continent. Layer imprudently visited him in Rome on the pretext of doing business for the Pastons of Oxnead. Kit gave the 'Pretender' a list of Norfolk gentry with a Tory leaning who he supposed might be 'Jacobites'. In return James offered to be God-Father by proxy at the baptism of Layer's daughter Clementine in London. Kit was betrayed by some of his confidents and he was arrested at his London home. He escaped but was soon recaptured in Lambeth and put into the Tower in chains. After a trial lasting 18 hours he was found guilty on five counts of treason. After a long delay he was horribly executed at Tyburn, in 1723 aged 40.

Other disasters; 1737, a small pox out-break; 1743, cattle plague. The population of Aylsham plummeted from 1320 in **1731**, to 990 in **1741**; a drop of a quarter. By **1751** the population recovered to 1230 but in **1757**, the harvest failed. **1776** a new work-house was built replacing the earlier poor-house and alms-houses near the river. It was only from 1790 onwards that the town's population began to rise steeply and by 1821 it doubled to the figure of 1741. This was mainly due to improved communications and the economic benefits that followed.

Early writers who visited Aylsham like Celia Fiennes in **1698** and Daniel Defoe (1660-1731) in **1732**, were complimentary. The Norfolk historian the Rev Francis

Blomefield visited the town in the 1730s. He wrote, 'Aylsham is in the most agreeable and pleasant part of Norfolk' and went on to list its attributes. Sir William and Lady Beauchamp-Proctor visited the Black Boys Inn in **1764**. They found it 'neat and tidy; very reasonably priced'. Lord Nelson danced in the large Assembly Room upstairs in the hotel in **1792**. Aylsham was by then the most fashionable place in North Norfolk to visit.

The population graph following, shows how little its size seems to have grown over an immense period of time. This changed dramatically from 1700 onwards during the agricultural revolution and then the industrial revolution. The century ended with yet another war with France. North Norfolk had to improve its agricultural performance, increasing its production and surplus for the cash market. Aylsham town centre hardly reflected any of these changes though Millgate and its industrial area in Dunkirk on the northern side of the river, continued to grow.

In the late 1700s there was a surge in population growth across north Norfolk and again in the boom years of High Victorian farming in the middle 1800s. From 1850 to 1950, for a complete century the population of Aylsham flat-lined. Then it went from the horizontal to the near vertical with exponential growth. Fortunately development has still not been on a scale sufficient to swamp the established character and scale of the town or to threaten its identity. Is it now on the tipping edge?

34) <u>Improvements in communications and public utilities.</u>

Stone, Hun, Mill, Wood, Drabble all have the name 'gate' appended to them because they were gated and carefully guarded by the town's bailiffs to stop vagrants coming from outside the parish to claim support and settlement. A settlement certificate was made for that purpose. This form of street name may date from Danish times (10th century) but 'gate' in itself does not mean a road. The meaning of other roads;
Bolwick – 'bull'; East Field, Furze Ground, Drabble = dirt/ mire, Hungate was recorded from 1257; Mermaid Beck, also called Aylsham Beck.
Millgate was recorded in 1624; Sankence, is a diminution of 'Samp-sons'. Richard Yaxley was recorded in 1644 (NA) but the name Yaxleys Way comes from a much later inhabitant. 'Woodgate' was mentioned in the court of the 'Fleet of Fines' in 1378.

The southern approach to the town centre was historically along a tree lined lane from Marsham. It entered the town via Hungate Street. This is narrow and has no pavements so a coach and four horses found it difficult to pass other on-coming vehicles. By the 1700s it had long been superseded by Norwich Road to the east. Cromer Road to the north of the town centre also has the character of a quiet country lane but it was not replaced with a by-pass until the 1980s.

One of the lost long distance routes to Aylsham led from Wolterton village in a south-eastern direction to a crossing (ford?) over the River Bure near the old Bishop's manor house in Blickling Parish. The southern part of this route still runs through Blickling Park west of the lake in the form of a track-way to the remnant of Blickling village. It continued in a south-eastern direction past the stately forecourt of the Hall; continuing on the northern side of the parish church and on towards Aylsham. In the 19th century the route was moved from the northern side of the churchyard to the south side.

The map of Norfolk surveyed by Thomas Donald and Thomas Milne was published by William Faden in **1797** (see the part showing Aylsham in the Appendix). It gives the earliest idea of the roads and track-ways around Aylsham. The map also shows the considerable area of heath-land to the south-west of Aylsham which was still not planted up with trees. A single, north to south road goes through it, already referred to. The large size of Blickling's park is also shown on the map. Ancient highways were rationalised through 'Road Orders'. Only three minor Road Orders are known from the late 1700s. They show only small modifications to the road layout in Aylsham parish.

The lack of an early Enclosure Map for Aylsham also inhibits us from working out how the road and lane network in the parish evolved. Much of it has to be guesswork. In **1794**, an Act of Parliament was passed, to provide a turnpike road between Norwich and Cromer via Aylsham. The new road was completed in 1796. The Napoleonic War made new and better roads necessary so that troops could move quickly around the countryside in the event of an invasion threat. Mail coaches could travel to London in a single day instead of two. Until then the parish was responsible for maintaining the king's highway – the *'regia via'* within their boundaries. This duty was confirmed by a Statute of 1555. Church Wardens appointed unpaid surveyors to supervise the works. The materials and labour were paid for from a special parish rate. Manorial courts upheld the law against impediments. The new Turnpike road to Aylsham and the same continuing northwards remained country lanes by modern standards for a very long time but at least they were better maintained after the 1790s. One of the surviving features of the Turnpike is the miles-stone of which several survive in and near the parish.

Aylsham has two bridges built close together. They lie on the northern side of the town. The so-called 'Great Bridge' still only has a single carriage width yet buses and coaches travel over it on a daily basis. The 'Little Bridge' (further north) was rebuilt after the canalisation of the River Bure by the same builder. Up to the 1790s the River Bure was only navigable westwards as far as Coltishall except in extreme weather conditions when there was flooding. The river was then canalised as far as a new basin, staithe and mooring in Dunkirk. New warehouses were built. This led to the expansion of Millgate with workshops, small industries and workers' houses when it became a large suburb.

The new canal called the 'Bure Navigation' was narrow but huge amounts of produce and goods were transported in *wherries* (flat bottomed sailing boats) to Great Yarmouth and beyond. This gave a short stimulus to the growth of population in Aylsham that lasted until the 1850s. This economic boom in Aylsham was at the cost of Coltishall and Horstead. They only regained their status as the head of the river after the great flood of 1912. This calamity destroyed several locks and the use of the canal then ended.

In **1772**, Henry Biedermann surveyed the River Bure in preparation for its canalisation. Part of the survey included the town centre of Aylsham. This is the earliest known survey of the town. It shows a compact town centre which had hardly changed for centuries. The built-up area covered a remarkably small area of about 30 acres. Heinrich Augustus Biedermann was the draughtsman and surveyor to Charles Duke of Brunswick 1760-65. He moved to London where he married an English girl. He became 'Henry' but he retained the German spelling of his surname – unless someone misspelt it for him! His meticulously drawn maps are minute in size. Did his eye sight survive into old age? After this major work in Aylsham he surveyed the vast Holkham estate and then the Gunton estate for Sir William Morden Harbord, Bart. That estate book is now in the Norfolk Record Office. Henry was only naturalised in 1804 and died in Tutbury, Gloucs in 1816.

See below, Henry Biedermann's survey map of Aylsham. The roads and buildings of the town centre are only shown diagrammatically – Hungate Street and its many early buildings are not shown for example. This is because the focus of the survey was the River Bure and the riparian ownerships of land either side of it. By comparison, the Survey Map of Norfolk published by William Faden (also in the Appendix) shows a lot more detail of Aylsham. It was surveyed about twenty years later than the Biedermann map. Unfortunately many of the road improvements partly through Road Orders had already taken place by then so it is difficult to be sure what existed before that development. Faden's map has been digitally enhanced to improve clarity and legibility.

In **1798**, the 'King's Water Mill on the south side of the river was rebuilt on a grand scale. Many new industries sprang up and the town supported a wide range of cottage based crafts which survived right into the 20th century. At last Aylsham had fulfilled its early promise of being a service centre for the surrounding district.

A report made in 1851 high-lighted the long term chronic drainage problem in Aylsham. This had been made much worse with the growth of industry next to the river. The report required as a temporary measure for cess pits and open drains to be covered. The big houses had brick-lined drainage channels but most houses did not. They all eventually drained into the river Bure whose water was anything but 'pure'!

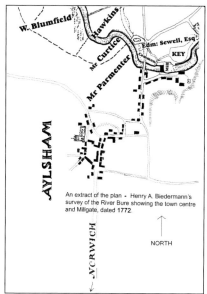

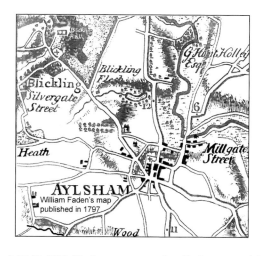

MAP (27) Fadens mpore detailed map published 25 years later.

MAP (26) Aylsham's earliest though rather diagrammatical survey map.

In 1938 fresh water was piped into the town and much of that was drained into the foul system which over-loaded it. It was not until 1952 that pail closets were replaced by flushed toilets. 7¾ miles of foul drains were built in the town. They flushed using gravity and flowed into a sewage treatment plant developed on 'Mucklands' meadow near the river.

35. A post-script on communications.

The railways were extended from Norwich to Aylsham in 1881 with a branch line westwards to Fakenham. Aylsham North Station was built in Dunkirk, the suburb on the northern side of the river. Aylsham South Station on the east side of Norwich Road served a branch line between Wroxham and a county school to the west. It was opened a year later. The North Station and its lines brought a wider area within reach than the old canal and to some extent it replaced it. The South Station and lines helped Aylsham to be better connected with the rest of the county and beyond. It was no longer a settlement that could be isolated in bad weather.

Both branch lines were closed under the Beeching Act in 1952/3 but the Wroxham Line was retained as the 'Bure Valley Railway'. This is a narrow gauge railway nine miles long and a tourist attraction. The former station has a large car park, railway shop, café and a small museum. In the opposite western direction the former track became a long distance footpath that winds its way to Cawston, Reepham and eventually to Norwich - 'Marriot's Way'. The eastern part of the line to the north of Aylsham has become the 'Weavers Way' - another long distance footpath. The negative effect on the ancient landscape was that the railway lines and later the by-pass highway carved up old farm holdings. The positive result was when the lines and buildings were cleared away they provided accommodation land for new industrial expansion and now Dunkirk is a large and thriving business estate close to the town centre but discretely separated from its residential neighbourhoods.

The A140 originally went through Aylsham town centre and Ingworth village until a by-pass was built to the east in 1980. Instead of crawling along to Cromer and back, vehicles could then drive up to 60mph so the pace of life in northern Norfolk certainly speeded up. This new road cut off the meadows on the east side of the parish. The by-pass continues on the south side of the parish towards Cawston and Reepham as the B1145. Before 1977 the southern part of the A140 Norwich Road was a narrow tree-lined lane running along the west side of the Bolwick estate. Much of it is still there for walkers and cyclists, running parallel to the modern road. Another road given a 'B' status was the B1354 between Blickling, through the town centre to Brampton and Coltishall to the south-east. This lane has now been reduced to a C-grade road. The B1145 discontinues when it meets the town by-pass and rather confusingly reappears to the north-east as the road to North Walsham. Despite all these road improvements, the road between Aylsham and North Walsham remains a winding country lane. With all these changes the district moved on into the later 20th century – but not Aylsham town centre. With its Conservation Area, so designated under Planning Law and many 'Listed Buildings' of historic value it has held on to its traditional character to the benefit of tourism and comfortable residential values.

37. Summary.

Pre-history bequeathed many features that have shaped the current landscape and even the town of Aylsham itself. It is probable that state and church came together to organise the landscape and its settlement in the early Anglo-Saxon period and it was that process that gave Aylsham its cultural centre-place status in the district around it. The parish church was more than a symbol but also the focal point culturally and physically in the town which it still is. It is indisputable that in the Middle Ages Aylsham did become an important estate centre. How much of the administration lay in the hands of the local aristocracy rather than the town itself can be argued. Aylsham has happily avoided being touched by war, bombing and battles during its long history even though there was a World War II airfield nearby at Oulton. This relative isolation has helped to nurture Aylsham's peaceful character to develop uninterrupted and in continuity, keeping a balance between conservation and the need for progressive development.

When Blickling Hall and its estate were handed over by the Marquis of Lothian to the National Trust in 1940, that gift included Aylsham town centre. New industry was introduced into the Dunkirk area north of the town and new residential suburbs developed on all four sides. The developed footprint of the town now extends to over a mile square, or 350 acres. This is smaller than most communities in Norfolk which often cover about a quarter of their parish. The plans shown in the Appendix offer a comparison between the extent of the built-up area 130 years ago and now, though some areas identified for future development have been added.

By understanding their origins, the historic market towns of Norfolk will be in a far stronger position to influence how the growth of settlements if it is needed is managed in the long term. There may be a case for arguing that this should not be determined only in a one-sided partnership dominated by central government but with the local community expressing their own needs with much strengthened delegated powers.

The juxta-position of the old and new maps shown below high-lights the amount of urban growth that has taken place in modern times. The earliest map showing the whole town was drawn by Henry Biedermann (see notes above) in 1772. Several parts of the town are omitted from the plan but it does give some idea of the compactness of the settlement. William Faden's map was published in 1797 but surveyed a few years before that and it gives a more accurate idea of the limited extent of the town at the end of the 18th century. Although the buildings of the town lined the main street there were several large houses in their own grounds. Also there was a multitude of land with yards, paddocks, orchards, storage, etc. These spread out over a much larger area than just the town centre.

The last historical map shown here is the earliest Ordnance Survey Map of 1885 published just over a century after Faden's map yet the built up part of the town was still compact except for the new suburb of Millgate and Dunkirk. The really big jump in expansion was at the end of the 20th century when the 'footprint' of the town multiplied several times. This reflected the fashion for low density 'garden suburbs'.

It has been said that 'there is a remarkable consistency of plan in Aylsham' where the spitit of 700 years has provided an organic model of organic growth difficult to parallel in England (taken from the *'Bure Valley Path'*, leaflet) which is probably what makes it Norfolk's premier market town.

MAP (28- 29) comparing the extent of urban development in 1839 and now. Next page -

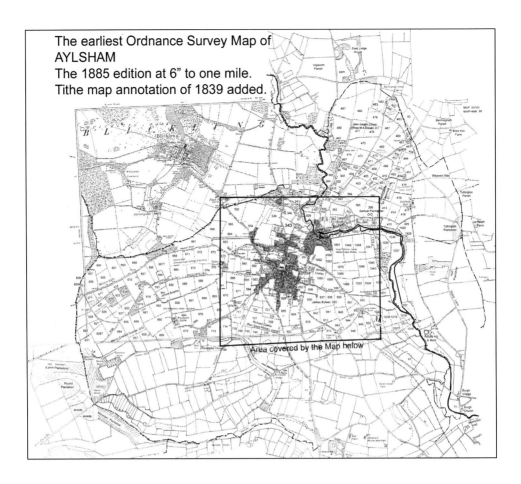

The earliest Ordnance Survey Map of
AYLSHAM
The 1885 edition at 6" to one mile.
Tithe map annotation of 1839 added.

Area covered by the Map below

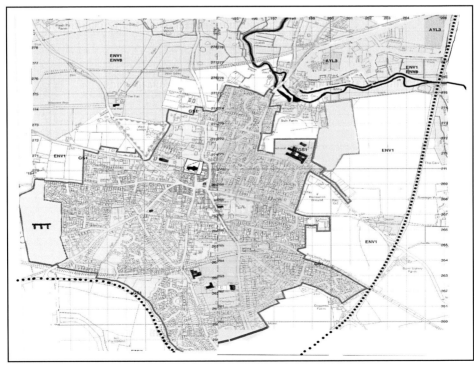

CHART (9) POPULATION

<u>Aylsham's estimated or published population figures;</u>

1050, from *Domesday* – 868 people

1086, same source -   828 people

1303 tax subsidy returns

1334 same.

1349 - 1444, tax mitigation due to the Black Death, of 15%, or a loss of 120 people to 700.

1524 &, 1597 Subsidy tax lists.

1524/ 1584,   muster lists of able bodies men

1643, 349 covenant signatures in Aylsham (75 of them unreadable), ie all adults aged over 14, or
       half the population 1643 Solemn League of the Covenant signatures – 349 names.

1664, 133 names paid tax on 385 hearths; plus say half that who were exempt – population estimate
       700 people.

1678, Poll Tax, £6-13s-0d, paid @ 1s per adult head = 133.

1700, about 1200 people (rcf., '*The Poor of Aylsham*'), Aylsham Local History Society' pubn 1995

1720, 100 families lived in Aylsham.

1730, about 1290 people (reference as above).

1740, 970 people, when poor relief became impotent.

1751; 1,230 (Ref; 'Aylsham's Inns', Elizabeth Gale 2001). 'Settled People' only were given support.

1760, 1070 people.

1770, 1100 people.

1787/9, Baptist Chapel was built

1801; 1,667; 120 families in 1800 (14 per household?); 1809, 332 houses;

1811, 1760 people and 356 dwellings (5 people per house)

1821; 1,853 or, 929 (Pigot's directory)

1831; 2,334 and 4,030 acres including 100 acres of woods; 350 of meadow and four manors (White's
       directory). Value of the vicarage, £ 17-19s-7d with the abbot's tithes from east of the river
       belonging to Canterbury.

1841; Riche's directory; 4,103 accessible acres plus 200 woods, 350 meadows
       White's directory, 2,448 population; 4,311 1/2 acres1851; 2,741 people; annual value £9,191.

1851; 2,741; annual value £9,191. 1858 value of the vicarage, £533 pa with tithes leased at £550.

1858 value of the vicarage, £533 pa with tithes leased at £550.

1861; 2,740 (Harrod's directory), 2,623 White's directory; Kelly's ditto.

1871 census; Harrod's 1872 directory - 2,800; Harrod's 1877 directory – 'about
       2,500'. Kelly's directory 2,502 rateable value £12,370.

1881; Kelly's - 2,674 people; 572 dwellings/ 581 families (4.6 pcr dwelling); value
         £11,612. The vicarage was worth £533 / pa in 1875.

1891; same source, 2,533; including 125 inmates and managers in the workhouse;
       Rateable value of the Parish - £10,343.

1901; 2,471 people and 581 dwellings; £10,816. The parish church had seating for 850 people. The
       vicarage was worth £290 pa. Parish value was £10,504 (Kelly's Norfolk Directory 1900).

1911; 2,627; including 12 managers ands 137 inmates in the workhouse; £11,488; area 4,305 acres
       including 25 water.

1921; 2,466; £12,083; Vicarage worth £480 pa. Places of worship; the Mission Room,
       1890; Baptist Chapel in White Hart Street seated 350; 1791 AD; Wesleyan Methodist Chapel;
       Reformed Wesleyan Chapel; Primitive Methodist Chapel was in Cawston Road. Gospel Hall;
       Catholic Chapel in a private house.

1931; 2,646; area - 2,646 acres. Vicarage annual value £641 – 5 acres of glebe.

1941, no census due to the Second World War

1951, 2,526 – a small drop since 1931

1961, 2,635

1971; 3,720 - a dramatic 40% rise in a decade

1981; 4,697 – a further rise of 26%.

1991, 4,955

2001; 5,420 – the town had more than doubled in size since 1961.

2011; 5,504

Census data above supplied by Stephen Durrant; Statistical Services, Norfolk County Council.

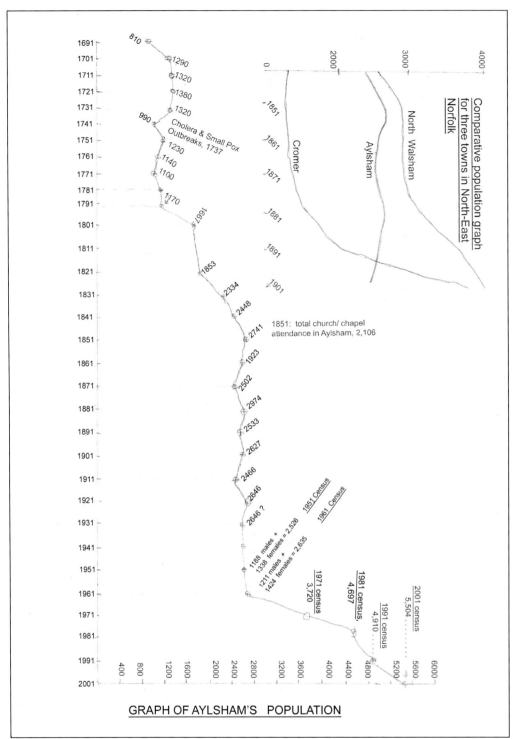

Comparative population graph for three towns in North-East Norfolk

Cromer

Aylsham

North Walsham

Cholera & Small Pox Outbreaks, 1737

1851: total church/ chapel attendance in Aylsham, 2,106

1691 — 810
1701 — 1290
1711 — 1320
1721 — 1380
1731 — 1320
1741 — 990
1751 — 1230
1761 — 1140
1771 — 1100
1781 — 1170
1791
1801 — 1657
1811
1821 — 1853
1831 — 2334
1841 — 2448
1851 — 2741
1861 — 1923
1871 — 2502
1881 — 2974
1891 — 2533
1901 — 2627
1911 — 2466
1921 — 2646
1931 — 2646 ?
1941
1951 — 1188 males + 1338 females = 2,526   **1951 Census**
1961 — 1211 males + 1424 females = 2,635   **1961 Census**
1971 — **1971 census,** 3,720
1981 — **1981 census,** 4,697
1991 — **1991 census** 4,910
2001 — **2001 census** 5,504

GRAPH OF AYLSHAM'S POPULATION

CHART (10) Population graph showing changes in modern times.

APPENDICES
Appendix (1)
1. <u>A selection of sites relating to Aylsham in the Norfolk Archaeology HER List;</u>

HER number;

2,796; the 'Fen Causeway'; a long distance Roman Road passing south of Aylsham towards Brampton

5,115; <u>Blickling Hall</u>, developed in the 14th c with a large moat and double courtyard. Originally a half-timbered building but rebuilt in brick in the late 15th c.

6,095; 7,545 and 12,773 – <u>several barrows</u> near the corner of Aylsham and Tuttington parish boundaries in the woods 2 miles east of Aylsham excavated in 1808 when 2 urns were found filled with bones and human ashes. Also a ceramic urn was ploughed up near Aylsham containing 500 silver coins of Henry VIIth's time. TG 2129-2534; and 2124-2525.

6,714; TG 1701-3029, Bishop's Old Hall in northern part of Blickling Parish next to the river. It was moated but no evidence of domestic buildings was found during excavations – was it only a farm? The long distance route from Wolterton to Aylsham went next to this site.
Norfolk Archaeology journal, vol 6, 341- 6; vol., 16, 147-152; vol 26, xli.

7,545; TG 2192-2741. Several barrows 18m diameter and one, 11 metres diameter.

7,463; TG 18,853-27457, <u>Aylsham Old Hall</u> 1689, altered between 1820-50.

7,563; TG 2069-2862; the <u>moated hall</u> of Abbot Sampson of Bury St Edmunds Abbey since 1190. Between 1570 and 1610 it was rebuilt and extended in 1706.

7,587; TG 2033-2435, Roman roof tiles found near Bolwick Hall – part of the remains of a <u>Roman Villa</u>. Also a rectangular enclosure and a lime-kiln. The site was excavated between 1939 and 1956.

7,588; TG 2010-2459, <u>Roman rubbish pits</u> near the above had finds of Samian pottery-ware from France.

7,657; TG 2010-2440, <u>Water Mill</u> near Bolwick Hall of 1889 ruined by 1965

11,541; 198-254, enclosure of a lost field.

11,542; same, north of Burgh Road.

12,213, 1915 x 2675, <u>Butt-lands</u> on the south side of the town. Used for archery practice at least since 1542.

12,219; <u>medieval chapel</u> (?) near 'Kirkland Field' in Dunkirk (northern Aylsham)? This is speculative.

12,772; TG 1701-3029; north of Abbot's Hall crossing the parish boundary into Erpingham. A large <u>hengi-form enclosure</u> like a Roman amphitheatre; 2 parallel features (ditches?) a mile long crossing the Aylsham by-pass and cut by a local road like an elongated square. Crop marks, 3 causeway enclosures; finds – a hearth, pot-boiler and Roman brooch etc.

12,773; TG 1710-2719; undated rectangular enclosure.

12,861, 2110 x 2787, <u>medieval hall-house</u> and later a 17th century, two storey farm house?

12, 982; 1731 x 2683, rectangular <u>enclosure</u> date unknown, between Heydon and Green Lanes.

13,479; 2003 x 2608, <u>Duggen's Farm</u> with a brick shaped gable 17th century.

14,940; 206 x 294; <u>Bronze Age-Iron Age settlement</u> between Ingworth & Banningham.

15,885, 1907 x 2664, a post medieval <u>windmill</u> unused after 1941; between Swan Close and Mill Road.

18,078; 2007 x 2601, south of Biggins Farm on the Aylsham by-pass.

18, 059; 2651 x 7410, another post medieval <u>windmill</u> north of the Cawston Road.

19,708, 2028 x 2637; a burnt mound.

19,894; 1925 x 2686; 16th century <u>Unicorn Inn</u> opposite Aylsham public Library.

20,549; TG 169-251, <u>Guy's Hill</u>, a Bronze Age barrow near Frog Hall and Stourtons Water.

21,849, <u>Roman marching fort</u> in Cawston identified on aerial photographs in 1996. A lost settlement has been identified on aerial photographs associated with the fort with crop marks of early field patterns nearby.

30,276; 1920 x 2557; <u>Spa Farm</u> near a 19thc, chalybeate spring and mineral spa used to relieve chronic illnesses. 17thc half-timbered house extended in the 1800s to accommodate people visiting the spa.

30,289; 1754 x 2675, lost <u>track-way</u> between Heydon Lane and Green Lane running parallel to them.

31,740, <u>Stowe Heath</u> (OS 23,322 x 26,896); south-east and near to Tuttington Church; with a long barrow showing distinctly in an aerial photograph. Six large pits at one end for post-holes perhaps; 2¼ miles east of Aylsham towards Church Lane.

33,592; TG 23/26, in Burgh-by-Aylsham parish, a <u>Roman-British Farm</u> with many finds; Roman furniture fitting, coins, brooch, Samian ware, harness fittings, stirrup, spoons, keys, knife, weight, pots, stud etc. Iron Age terret.

36, 460; TG 2052-2626; ring ditch, Bronze Age?

36,461; south-east of Ingworth Church could be the site of <u>Ingworth Hall</u> on the border with Aylsham parish. This area of carr next to the river could be just drainage ditches and not a medieval moat. There is another

potential site for two moats on the western side of Tuttington by the river but also likely to be just as above 36,463; TG 2135-2571, crop marks of a great house on the western side of the River Bure.
41, 037 leading north-eastwards to the coast in the area of Mundesley – Happisburgh.

2. <u>Written and other references to archaeology.</u>

Norfolk Archaeology journal, vol 41, 365; a Roman vessel showing an escutcheon (with a bust?) bucket fitting. Early Anglo-Saxon annular brooch and wrist clasp found in Aylsham.
NA 42, 391; a Roman cast vessel handle with a lobe.
    Excavations for the Aylsham by-pass, report awaited from Gregory & Percival; p229, the finds included a 14[th]c seal matrix with a falcon or hawk, an EAS cross brooch etc.
<u>Woodgate House.</u> Peter Purdy reported many archaeological small finds in a field east of the Nursery near Cawston Road a Roman kiln was found in 2014. Also a 40 by 30 metre ditched enclosure that looked Iron Age south of the house. The lake in the grounds form the head water for Mary's Beck which flows south into Mermaid's Beck. Was this another Roman villa? None of these items have yet been listed in the County Archaeology HERs list.
The new housing estate next to the old Workhouse, south-west of the town was cleared of top-spoil prior to construction and one find was made – a Bronze Age funeral <u>beaker</u> for cremated remains (anecdotal report).
Iron Age bronze coin found in Aylsham and an EAS cruciform brooch in the fields.

The Roman town of Brampton.

East Anglian Archaeology, no 5. Report on the excavations of 1973-74.
This site has been known since Sir Thomas Browne published in 1667, his find of Roman Urns in an arable field between Brampton and Buxton, near the edge of Oxnead Park. A modern road crosses the site of the Roman town with 5 Ha on one side and 2½ Has, on the other. The fort was large enough to house an entire legion. In the post-Flavian period its defensive ditches were partly filled in but they were still 2 meters deep.

    Prehistoric finds were also made but there is no evidence that the site was occupied before the 1[st]c. The archaeology showed that the fort was built by the military just before or after Boudicca's rebellion in AD 70. The 'playing card' corners of the fort's defences are less rounded than usual which gives doubt about its exact date. Domestic occupation later took over the site. No roofing tiles were found. The buildings seem to have had timber-framed walls with wattle and daub panels and thatched roofs. Potters and smelters occupied the fort area with homes and workshops. Pots were fired in the extensive kiln-field west of the fort where there were far fewer buildings. The former have been found on Hadrian's Wall which suggests much of the output shipped down the river to Caister was intended for the Roman Army. The decoration of the pottery is similar to that of Lincolnshire-ware. Production intensified in the 2nd and 3rd centuries. It continued into the 4[th]c after production in other regions had declined. A lot of water was needed to produce pottery. The water-table is only 3.15 metres below the surface so many wells were dug and heavily lined with timber – some nearly 7 metres deep. When excavated these produced a wide variety of Roman artefacts. Several clay pits were found – pottery clay was probably sourced from a wide area. There were also a temple, bath house etc in the town.

    The old course of the River Bure came further south and near to the Fort where there was a staithe and perhaps store-houses. A railway now runs through the site of the Fort so there are two bridges to allow roads to pass under the line. Two Roman roads led northwards. The north-western road now leads south to Coltishall (B1354). The northern-eastern part of this road, close to the centre of Aylsham joins with Norwich Road.

Appendix (2)   <u>Key dates in history that affected East Anglia.</u>

New Stone Age (2500-1200 BC) flint axes & arrow heads; is evidence found in Aylsham of hunter-gathers who gradually turned to cultivation.
Bronze Age (1200-300 BC) a shift from cultivation to herding of livestock. Long distance track-ways and burial mounds followed.
Iron Age (300BC – 43 AD) small temporary encampments with 'celtic fields' rather than co-axial fields found in north-east Norfolk. By the end of this period farming had evolved over a period of 2,000 years.
Anglo-Saxons; in the 6thc AD the 'great migration' of peoples began. They travelled from the north-west continent to England and especially into East Anglia.

917, King Edward re-conquered East Anglia from the Danes and 60 years of peace followed.

952-6, a new diocese was created in the region with North and South Elmham being the bases in Norfolk and Suffolk respectively. These were in villages. Eadwulf was its first bishop in over 80 years. Norwich and Ipswich flourished as new ports. Suburbs spread over the old ditches and ramparts which were levelled.

978, King Edgar II, 'the unready' became king when still a boy. Civil war followed.

980, In Scandinavia conversion to Christianity began so pagans from those countries roamed the high seas. Viking raids were renewed along the coast of East Anglia.

991, Ipswich was ravaged.

1002, the Danes were slaughtered everywhere except in East Anglia where they a strong foothold. The sister of Svein King of Denmark was killed during this ethnic cleansing programme so he invaded England.

1004, Norwich was sacked and then Thetford. The Saxon leader, Ulketel ordered their ships to be burnt but that did not happen and the Danes escaped.

1009, Svein returned and occupied Ipswich. He won the Battle of Ringmere, near Thetford.

1012, Svein became King of England so Ethelred King of Wessex fled into exile. Svein died soon afterwards. His son Canute inherited the throne of Denmark and after 1028, Norway as well.

1015, Canute invaded England and won the Battle of Abingdon in Essex. Edmund 'Ironside' remained King of Wessex and agreed to eastern England becoming 'Danelaw'.

Appendix (3) Key dates in the history of Aylsham

1086, Domesday Survey

1329, by then, Aylsham linen also called 'AylshamWebb' and the 'Cloth of Aylsham' was woven in the town by Flemish weavers. It was even exported up to the 16th c.

1488, Richard Howard, Sheriff of Norwich and his wife Cecilia endowed the raising of the south porch with a *parvis* chamber above. Their effigies in brass shows them in linen shrouds.

1490, St Peter's guild in the north transept. The Rev Thomas Tylson BA, is shown in a brass wearing an amice with scrolls. Another sepulchre brass of this date shows Robert & Katherine Forman.

1507, panels in the screen painted paid for by Thomas Wymer, worsted-weaver.

1530. Robert Jannys, was born in Aylsham and became Sheriff of Norwich in 1509; Mayor of Norwich in 1517 and 1524. He left £10 in his Will to buy land which would generate rent to pay a school-master; and also for masses to be said. This established a 'free' grammar school near the churchyard for seven free scholars. The endowment was too small to pay the teacher. He had to be supported by subscription.

1573, Robert Harrison was the teacher there even though he was notorious for his bad temper. The bishop and others opposed his appointment. The original school house was demolished and rebuilt in 1792, and extended in 1814.

15.. Archbishop Parker endowed two places in Cambridge University for pupils of Aylsham & Wymondham.

1543, a Bridewell was built by Robert Marsham, squire of Stratton Strawless on the corner of Burgh Road and Red Lion Street.

1600, a new pulpit was placed in the parish church.

1603, linen weaving was replaced by wool for waistcoats, stockings and knit wear.

1614/1622, a list of tenants was made for Aylsham Lancaster Manor.

1638, Thomas Cressey set up a trust for the poor to be housed in Smithson's & Gikes Cottages.

1653, the earliest surviving church registers began. A fair was held each 23rd March and the last Tuesday in September.

1673, the Town Meadow was given to Aylsham. It was sold in 1856.

1730, cottages and land given for the poor by Simon Porter who was also the Lord of the Manor in 1739.

1737, a small-pox outbreak in the town.

1743, cattle plague

1757, the harvest failed.

1773 an Act of Parliament allowed Aylsham to build the Bure Canal between Coltishall and Aylsham for boats up to 40 tons.

1776, the new workhouse was built. By 1800 it had 40 - 50 inmates; in 1832 there were 75 - 90.

1779, the canal was finished at a cost of £6,000 for boats with a draft up to 2½ feet. This included a wharf and basin near the bridge north of the town centre. The suburb of Millgate expanded. Stone, coal, corn, and timber were carried and boat-building begun. Machinery elsewhere displaced the cottage textile industry of Aylsham.

1789, the Bridewell was rebuilt. Nicholas Burgeys was convicted of hitting with a cudgel the constables who were trying to arrest him in Aylsham Market Place (date unknown). He was a notorious poacher of hares in the Fields of Aylsham. Fined 20d, and he seems to have been whipped.

1798, Aylsham Mill was built. It remained in operation until 1969.

1805, there was a parade of soldiers in Aylsham Market Place led by the Rev Major (!) John Collyer, who commanded the 'Loyal Aylsham Light Infantry Volunteers'. After the parade he conducted a service in the parish church.

1814, a subscription paid for an enlargement of the school – 50 boys and 50 girls were there by 1836.

1818, a Savings Bank was established at the school with £18,000 deposited by local people.
24th March, Humphrey Repton the famous landscaper died. A large memorial to his memory was placed in a fenced enclosure by the parish church chancel.

1828, when Norwich Prison was built, Aylsham's primitive old Bridewell was closed after only 39 years.

1836, the old Poor Union was replaced by Aylsham Poor Law Union. Architect William J. Donthorn designed a new Tudor style 'palace' for 600 inmates. It was completed by 1848 and served a large area. It still exists west of the town between Commercial Way (now, Bure Way) and New Road but it has been converted into luxury homes. The new Union covered a large district in and around Aylsham.

1839, a Medical Club gave mutual support for members in and around Aylsham.

1840, the Choral Society met in the Concert Room, Red Lion Street.

1842, the old workhouse was replaced on the completion of the new Poor Law Union building.

1842-4, stained glass windows were placed in the chancel; and in the north and south aisles.

1848, a new school was built at a cost of £700.

1849, a gas works was built on Gas Lane, Millgate on the north side of the town costing £1500.

1850, there was a regatta in the summer on the Bure; a horticultural society; Blickling Park was open for walkers; a bowling green was provided in the town. Aylsham's public amenities were greatly expanded.

1852, the parish church was restored. New pews were placed inside.

1855, a cemetery was opened on two acres of land on Norwich Road.

1859, 'C' Company of the Norfolk Rifle Volunteers had 60 male volunteers in Aylsham.
The Corn Exchange was built in the Market Place. The shop opposite, Clarkes already had its elaborate and elegant window frontage.
A Police Station in Blickling Road had 2 sergeants and 15 Police Constables. The Aylsham District Police Station served 50 parishes and 47,853 people.
The Star Coach travelled between Cromer – Aylsham – Norwich and stopped at the Black Boys Inn in the Market Place. The former stables occupied the narrow yard at the rear.

1868, there was a reduction in agricultural wages so trade unions developed. Mr Applegate of the Blickling Brickyard was a union leader. The owners of the big landed estates around Aylsham felt their authority was threatened and thought Unions were divisive so they refused to recognise them.
Railway branch lines were opened from Aylsham to Norwich/ North Walsham to the east; Fakenham/ Reepham to the west

1883, a Savings Bank set up in the school had £23,000 of deposits made by 730 people. Street lights were placed on the highways.

1892, the Town Hall was extended and took over the remainder of London House on it west side.

1900, the Queen's Jubilee was celebrated. A dinner was provided for all the residents of the town in the Market Square.

1911; a new organ was placed in the parish church. 1913, the Soame Pump was opened in a public ceremony.

1922; Lt Col H. Bowman lived in the Manor House; the Rev John Hoare was the vicar.

1929, the town's gas lights in the streets were superceded by electricity.

1930, by then local trades had shrunk – no more shoe-making, tanners, millers, cattle cake and artificial manure manufacture were found in Aylsham. The canal and water-mill became disused and derelict.

1931, Aubrey Bowman was living in the Manor House; Mrs P. Shepheard lived at Abbot's Hall.

1938, water was piped to houses who could then abandon their yard privies and instal internal bathrooms.

1950, Dr Richard Beeching closed the north and south railway lines and stations. The latter became the Bure Valley (miniature) railway and the other line became the 'Weaver's Way', a long distance footpath.

Appendix (4) Ancient Woodland in north-east Norfolk.

Aylsham and North Walsham are in the Loam Soil Region of Norfolk which extends northwards to the coast and south to Norwich. To the east are the Broads; to the south-west, is Mid Norfolk; to the west is the Sands region. Loam soils are very fertile. It is often thought that the Loams supported many villages. In the Domesday Survey north-east Norfolk was densely settled but the Boulder Clay region of South Norfolk had even more villages – its fertile soils are more consistently spread across the landscape. In the Loams area there are many areas of sand and gravel which were covered by heaths.

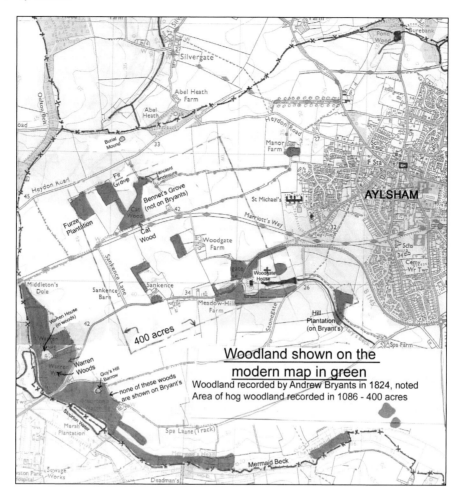

MAP (30) <u>Aylsham's modern plantations</u>

There was a general reduction of woodland in Norfolk between 1066 and 1086. Examples of the reduction in the woods of the South Erpingham Hundred at that time; Blickling, 200 – 100 pig woods; Buxton, 1000 – 200; Cawston, 1500 – 1000; Aylsham 400 – 300; Mannington 60 – 30. The conservation of these woods in the Iron Age when timber became increasingly scarce is perhaps the only indicator available to us that managed estates were in existance when the Romans arrived.

Tom Williamson (UEA) has said it is unlikely that there was much woodland management in Norfolk before the Middle Ages. Most of the town's need for osiers, fencing and lathed mud walls in buildings was probably sourced from the riverside meadows. Aylsham has nearly four miles of river frontage along the Bure; another four miles along the Mermaid Beck and a mile along Marys Beck. Most of the building timber traditionally came from hedgerow trees rather than woodland where competition between trees meant they were usually small in growth compared to those around fields. Most of the hedgerows in Aylsham have survived unlike in other parts of Norfolk where industrialised farming has led to a 'prairie' landscape.

Appendix (5) Items of historic interest in the parish church

1. '*Norfolk Rood Screens'*, P. Hurst & J. Hoselock; Phillimore pubn 2012.

The chancel screen symbolically marked the transition from the physical life where its imagery was over-whelming, to the next stage of wisdom where a more spiritual life lay. This point of change was under the chancel arch. Above the screen hung the rood cross with Jesus flanked by two women from scripture; hence the name 'rood screen'. The screen in Aylsham is comparable with those in the churches of Marsham, Worstead and Cawston as all four screens are painted in the same style and perhaps by the same artists. The earliest panels in Cawston were probably made by itinerant painters from the Norwich School of artists and painted about 1460. Then came the first eight panels on the north side in 1480; the screen doors in 1492-4. These were done sitting on the floor and painting directly onto the panels.

Image (23)

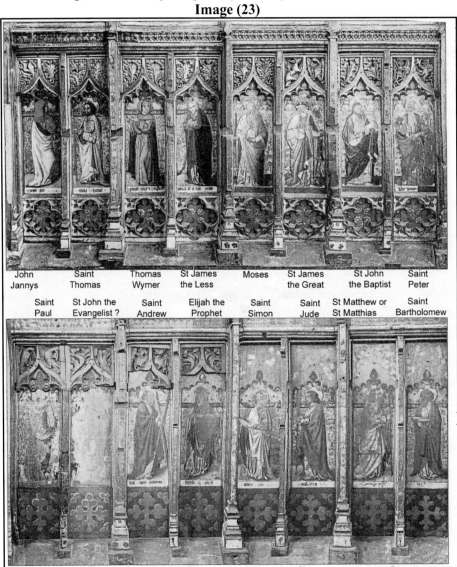

a view of the entire chancel screen panels and their current identification.

They are separated by a central aisle with the northern section of the screen at the top; the southern part at the bottom.

Woodcuts and engravings from Germany, Flanders and other parts of the Continent then became available to the Norwich artists. A more sophisticated style was introduced to Cawston about 1510. Also paper could be laid onto a table and be painted before being cut out and stuck into the panels. In the composition, light was used to articulate the folds in drapery. Sideways poses of the figures also gave them a stronger form. Hands and feet were painted with increasing skill. The juxta-positioning of the old and new styles of painting is quite dramatic. Two phases of painting can also be seen in the panels of Aylsham Church. The panels of Aylsham were damaged more than those in Cawston but ten surviving panels were painted to a high standard.

'*Norfolk Churches*', 1911 pubn; J. Charles Cox, vol 1, 140-141. The subjects of the panels were identified in notes hand-written into the book by Dom Bede Camm, BA Oxon; of St Benets, Cambridge; and later, of Downside Abbey, Somerset (he was an expert on the Catholic period of church history). On his visit of 28 June 1930, he noted; 'Apostles' are shown under-lined – several are missing. Screen panels from the north to south;

1. Wife of the donor? A beardless figure that almost turns its back to us looking right and the face is only seen partly in profile. A richly patterned tunic with a blue cloak under a larger white cloak. Hair covered up.
2. The male donor. A sophisticated figure with a black chin beard wearing a light blue cloak but revealing an elaborate golden under-garment from the waist downwards. He holds a tall thin red staff. A golden pattern background to the figure and leaves in the spandrels. Abbreviated text below – '*pro animabius*' pray for the soul of Thomas (Wymer, worsted weaver).
3. The donor? – a figure without a halo in 15th century dress holding a sheaf of papers. A wide red band around his head; wearing a light brown cloak and another broad red band round his shoulders; over a black open necked shirt. Angels (if they existed?) gone. He is making a sign with his left hand? Text below . . .?
4. St James minor. He faces left has a grey beard. He is shown wearing a dark brown cloak. No angels survive but a horizontal band as below. He holds a stick which bends at the bottom and he holds an ornamental bag. Leaves in the spandrels. Text, black on white below; 'weaver'.
5. Moses, a bearded man with Satan sitting on his head wielding a sword. Moses wears a light blue cloak. He has an open book in his left hand and a staff in his right hand. The left angel is grimacing at the Devil. Leaves in the spandrels. The format and style is similar to panel (6).
6. St James major, with a pilgrim's hat and scallop shell emblem. A unicorn and pelican in the spandrels.
7. St John the Baptist, facing half right wearing a blue cloak; angels and gold band the same as in panel (8). He is shown holding a bible with a haloed lamb sitting on it, its head turned towards the apostle. Large leaves in the spandrels.
8. St Peter, with the long keys of heaven, resting on his left shoulder. He wears a long red cloak. His right hand holds a clasped book of the gospels. His bearded head has a sunburst halo. Behind his head is a broad horizontal band with two angels above it. Either side of his body are trees drawn in black lines on gold. In the spandrels is a dragon right; St George mounted and with a shield, left.

Doors to the chancel (gone) but the painted patterns on the reveals remain. Hinges also gone.

9. St Paul. In very poor condition – highly mutilated during the Reformation. He holds the richly decorated scabbard of a sword resting on his left shoulder. An angel is on either side of his head. Griffins in the spandrels (modern restorations?).
10. Subject unknown. The image has mostly gone but angels either side of the (lost) figure. Leaves in the spandrels.
11. St Andrew, his face gone. He holds a long thin diagonal Cross on the right side and he also looks right. He wears a dark cloak. Most of this panel has also been erased. Two griffins in the spandrels also look modern. Text on the base; '*has opis demnan*?'
12. A prophet? The figure has mostly gone. He wears a richly patterned golden cloak. Text, '*facet qui obit* '? Leaves in the spandrels.
13. St Simon, with a fish. He wears a light blue cloak revealing his shoulders and arm in a richly patterned golden under-garment. Text, '*animabius . . . . .* '? Pray for the soul of . . . . .
14. St Jude, with an oar.
15. St Matthias, with an axe.
16. St Bartholomew, with a knife.

The southern panels are in a poor condition – the northern panels are better preserved. St Michael and a dragon are shown in the spandrels above St Peter. Angels hold up the drapery of each figure. St Jude is in a striking red robe. His was an advanced form of portraiture and a sideways pose in the new Continental style. The background is a rich golden pattern including his halo and vest. This dates from **1507** when the worsted weaver John Wymer left money in his Will.

2. Other church items.

1. There are 17 stained glass windows; 6 in the south aisle, 3 more in its eastern extension, 1 in the north transept. 2 in the chancel (east & south), one at the west end of the south aisle to Humphrey Repton and one at the west end/north side of the north wall. Also one in the west window of the middle part of the tower. Small fragments of late Medieval glass are incorporated in the south chancel window.
2. In the Chancel, collegiate seats medieval style (19thc?) with high arms; 3 + 5 face the aisle each side; 4 each side face east; 24 in all for the choir.
3. Ledger slabs, some with armorial bearings partly hidden under the pews described above. From the west,
    1. John Jermy of Bayfield, Marion, Samuel; William Stark, *militus* MD, William Jermy etc.
    2. Rev Jonathan Wrench, vicar
    3. John . . .   of Swanton Morley, Nfk; Frances his wife who died 1766 aet 83; . . . .Thompson, . . . Saunders of Tewksbury, died 1820. No shield.
    4. John Jermy, Jane his wife, John . .
    5. Another John Jermy, of Bayfield.
    6. Elizabeth wife of Joseph Eldon, d 1726, 63; he died 1724 aged 52. No shield.
    7. others on the north side
    8. John Repton, head of the Excise Department in Norwich collector of revenues from eastern Norfolk and northern Suffolk. He married Martha Fitch. They were the parents of the landscaper, Humphrey Repton who was born in Bury St Edmunds. The Family lived there until they moved to Norwich. John Adey senior and junior are listed on the same slab. This memorial is in the south aisle.
4. The refurbishment of the church in 1852 cost £1600. The 'nave was cluttered with box pews and church Furniture'. They were replaced by the present pews, a reading desk, smaller pulpit etc.

3. The Aylsham Church Font.   **Image (24)**

Norfolk Archaeology vol 2, 83; by the Rev E T Yates. In the 17[th]c, a heavy 'baptistery' canopy was hung over the Font which was still there in 1847 but has now gone. Had it survived the canopy would now be regarded as an important historic feature of the church. The stone bowl has carved on its sides;

1/ pillar, cords, thorns (instruments of the Passion);
2/ the eagle of St John;
3/ a crucifixion (mutilated);
4/ the winged bull of St Luke;
5/ a spear crossed with a rod with a sponge at its end.

Below; angels with expanded wings and winged hearts.
On the stem, front – the arms of John of Gaunt for his munificence (?) arms of Morley and Bouchier on the sides;
HIS (for 'Jesus') on the rear side.

The height is 3'-6". The height of the steps was reduced in the Victorian period which harmed its composition says the Rev.Yates.

4. Visitations to Aylsham by Bishops of Norwich.

Norfolk Archaeology vol 28, 79; 'An Episcopal visitation in 1593 by Bishop Scambler' by Rev J F Williamson; p140; Christopher Roo of Aylsham was also listed under Gaywood as a witness to the sequestration.
Norfolk Record Society, vol 18, Bishop Redman's visitation, 1603; Deanery of Ingworth, p69; – only seven churches listed, and not Aylsham, hopefully because it was above criticism.

5. Clergy benefices

Norfolk Record Society, vol 32, p297, Aylsham, John Hunt vicar, King; 47s-3½d, 10ths; 3s-4d in synods; 7s-7½d procurations; in 1612, John Firmary (son of the former Vicar?) was amongst others issued with armour (corselettes).

p177; Roman Catholics in Aylsham – Thomas Smith & Charles Ratcliffe in 1604; five others in Brampton.

p131, 1604, silver plate belonging to the parish church worth £102-13s-4d in Aylsham; £23 in Blickling and £43-2s-6d in Cawston was to be sold off on the instructions of the Lord Protector the Duke of Somerset (in 1552?).

p56; John Bury, clerk was allowed to hold both of the benefices of Aylsham and Marsham churches in 1554. (1537-1608 records).

Bishop John Jegon found the air of Norwich 'too thin and sharp'. He preferred to live in Cambridge where it was thicker and . . . . he bought the manor house of Aylsham before his house in Ludham burnt down. He died there on 13 March,1618 leaving children Joan, Dorothy, Robert and John for whom he left no preferments in his £400 Will. His widow Dorothy married 2ndly Sir Charles Cornwallis, the former ambassador to Spain.

1535, The Vicar's manor was small but valued at £24-2s-8d . This included ¾ acre which was in Drabblegate (the Vicar's Mill?) and land containing mainly the alms-houses.

6. Bequests made in medieval Wills to the Church

NA 38, 276; '*Medieval parish church building in Norfolk*' Paul Cattermole& Simon Cotton. Bequests made to Aylsham Church;

1372-99, John of Gaunt, Duke of Lancaster owned the capital manor of Aylsham between 1372-99, and was the patron of the reconstruction of this church.

1377, John Eppe left a bequest for the furnishing of the chapel of the Holy Trinity in the north transept.

1379, Robert de Aylsham left money for a window in the chapel of the BVM.

1412, the great western tower of Cawston Church collapsed in a great gale.

1421, a bequest of 20s by an Aylsham man was made for the rebuilding of the tower.

1471, Katherine wife of Robert Purdy left funds for a lamps over the high altar; over the Holy Rood Cross in the chancel arch; the Chapel of BVM and a Plough Light; and other legacies for the Fraternity (Guild) of St Michael.

1479, Nicholas Purdy left 40d, to build the chapel (south transept) in Aylsham Church dedicated to the BVM. John Northawe left a legacy for lamps to St John the Baptist and St Peter's images; to the BVM and a black altar cloth.

1482, John Dowe left 12d, to build the same.

1483 (when the Cawston tower was finished?) there was a bequest of 10 Marks from Aylsham for a new bell.

1488, Richard Howard, Sheriff of Norwich left money then (he died in 1499) to increase the height of the south porch to provide a '*parvis*' chamber.

1495, Margaret Portland left money to pave the floor in front of the rood screen with marble.

1506, the Rev John Boller left money for 32 marble tiles to be placed around his father's grave stone in Aylsham Church as well as a pair of organs in the chancel near the chapel of the BVM.

1507, Thomas Wymer and his wife left money for the painting of the chancel screen and the painted canopy decoration on the roof timbers above it.

1512, William Rushborough of Coldham Hall left that place to his widow and a 'fodir' of land to pay £4 annual rent for a chantry priest in Aylsham Church.

1516, Joan Bell left money for a stone window-frame and glazing in the south wall of the south transept. Thomas Alleyn of Lyng left money for the fitting out of the chapel of the BVM.

1547, 3 cwts of church plate were sold off weighing 22 x 20 ounces for £102-13s-4d by church wardens, William White, Henry Drury and Henry Oliver. Twenty witnesses signed the document of sale. The money was used to repair the Great Bridge of Aylsham and six alms-houses.

7. Church Bells in Aylsham

1529, John Betts bequeathed £10 for a treble bell for the parish church.

1552, at the sequestration of church goods, five bells were declared.

1648 John Brend of Norwich made the great bell.

1699/ 1700, the large bells 5 & 6, were converted into 8 smaller chiming bells, by Samuel Gilpin of Norwich

1707, a treble bell was supplied by Thomas Newman of Norwich.

1726, no 6, bell was recast by John Stephen

1741, no 7, bell was re-cast by Thomas Newton? Four treble bells were supplied by Thomas Osborne & Edward Arnold of St Neots, Hunts.

1753, the peel of 8 bells was increased to 10.

The present church bells are as follows;

1 and 2, cast in 1775; 3, 4, 5, 10, cast in 1700; 6, in 1677 and given by Richard Howard; 7, in 1677 and recast in 1860; 8, in 1726; 9, in 1741; also a *Sanctus* Bell.

During the Napoleonic Wars the church bells were rung in celebration of the victories at the Battle of the Nile (1798), Trafalgar (1805) and Waterloo (1815).

8. Indent brasses and memorials

Reference; *Norfolk Archaeology*, vol 26, 'an 18thc record of Norfolk sepulchre brasses', H. O. Clark.

Those brasses listed by Francis Blomefield are;

1 / 2. Richard Howard, 13.1. 1499; his wife Cecily 1482. In the east end of the north aisle, both shown as grinning skeletons in winding sheets (this survives)

3. Alice Howard; 7 July1482, to their daughter?

4. Margaret Howard, his 1st wife, widow of Edward Cutler, Sheriff of Norwich, who died 20.12.1483.

5. John Howard, 30 August 1505

6. Margaret wife of Richard Harvey, no date.

7. Robert & Katherine Farman, no date (this survives)

8. Frengh, the brother of Thomas, Vicar here, 1418-29.

9. John Howard, 1495.

10. Robert & Marion Newman

11. Robert & Marion Orwell

12. Robert & Margaret Portland; he was Mayor of Norwich in 1477.

13. John & Agnes Jannys. He died in 1460.

14. Thomas Wymer, died 4 June 1507. This also survives.

15. Rev Thomas Tylson, BA; in the south part of the Sanctuary, Vicar 1490 - c1520; shown hands clasped and wearing an Amice (a strip of decorative cloth worn during mass), with curving scrolls rising from his shoulders,. See C Hugh Bryant, page 27, for the inscription.

16. Rev John Furmary, BA Cantab, no date; and his wife Margery was murdered 28.10.1522 aged 74 (born in 1448)

17. Robert & Margaret Hakin.

18. John de Bedford and his wife.

IMAGES (25 - 29)

Richard & Cecilia Howard, 1499

Robert & Katherine Farman

Rev Thomas Tylson

Rev John Furmary, BA; Vicar; north part of the Sanctuary

(right) Thomas Wymer, 1507.

9. <u>Extracts from the Aylsham Church Warden's accounts;</u>

Reference, NRO, MF 717.9/ PD 602/70.73

Aylsham Church is unusual in that on the wall of the south aisle is displayed a list of all the church-wardens dating back to the 1600s.

1635, the date of the earliest accounts surviving.

1640, Henry Robinson & John Neve, wardens, Rate charged to the town, £5-13s-8d
Total receipts, £26-13s-7d. Total disposed,   £26-13s-7d
Paid to Richard Curtis for breaking the church ground (grave digger),   6s-0d
Use of the town stock, to same, paid,   19s-2d
A load of straw for poor houses, paid 10s Thaxter (thatcher?)'s work, for bindings etc paid 19s-0d.
      Signed, John Durant, William Doughty, Thomas Green, Robert Bunn, John Green, John Brady,
          John Jireish,   Thomas Allen, John Andrews, Christopher Sankey.

1641, £21-16s-1d, received by the rates £43-2s-4d, plus £20-19s-1d from other sources and £1-4s-0d from Roger Spurver; £46-0s-10d received in total.
Paid out – for the 'causcy' (road-way) to the Little Bridge, mended by Nicholas Holmes, 11s-6d.
Ringers (of the church bells) on coronation day paid 6s. Bell ropes bought (a frequent item). Many payments were made to the poor but there was a much shorter list of disbursements than previously. £43-2s-4d was paid out in total.

1643 (the year of the market place demonstration) – no records for this year were found.

1644, Repair of the two bridges situated on Millgate Street; and mending the north stile in the church(yard) part paid by inhabitants and the 'out-dwellers' who use the Lands in the (Common) field;
£5-1s-7d, part of the rates taxed to the said town. £1 5s paid for the relief of the poor.

1644 & 1645. Charges in two separate rates, a total of £33-8s-6d (a big increase).

1646. Total charges, £36-16s-6d; discharged (payments) £34-8s-10d. £2-15s-8d (remained), signed William Doughty, John Riches, Robert Humphrey.
For 38 planks laid at the bridge at the old Market, 6s-4d, paid. Paid workmen for laying 33 feet of the same at the Great Bridge, 5s -6d. Work at the Bridewell, 8d.

1648, charges, £39 4s 4d   made on 25 April
          £58 13s 6d   another made in May
          £19 16s 5d
          <u>£34 1s 1d</u>
          <u>£3   8s   0d</u> rate for the poor
     155   3   4 + 29 3 0 = £184 6 4d, a huge jump up)

1662, accounts by Robert Burr & Robert Russell. Payments for; general income, £13-14s-0d
A new Common Book of Prayer, 7s   from the rates, £34--1s- 4d
Ringing for the king's burial,   10s-6d   rent from the Buttlands,   10s-0d
Rope for the Gabriel (bell)   1s-6d   for digging a grave,   6s 8d
Mending the gull at the Little Bridge,   6s-0d
etc   £48-12s-10d
                                                                      Total spent, £48-12s-0d

1696, receipts £127-3s-10d (another huge jump up) for a 14 monthly rate
1697, Philip Yaxley was paid 2s for . . .
etc

11. <u>Further notes on the Church.</u>

The arcade of the nave leans outwards by 14". Were the round piers recycled from the earlier church? The different periods of building can be seen on the outside of the church by looking at the variety of flint work – some are irregular, others coursed; some shaped, others random.
The glazing of the east <u>chancel window</u> dates from **1842-5** and shows the four favourite Disciples.
The sacred crowned monogram of the BVM can still be seen in the south Transept painted on the roof beams.
There is a small piece of old glass picturing St John in the south chancel window.
<u>Roof bosses</u> are carved with an eagle, child, flower, shield, a naked wild-man with a club.
The stalls in the chancel have carvings of the 12 apostles instead of poppy-heads.
The northern section of the <u>chancel screen</u> survived because a heavy pew was placed next to it in the 1640s. Underneath the painted panels was a continuous Latin text running along the whole base with 21 words including the dedication to its patron William Wymer. Gesso was applied to the faces of the figures; to the buttresses and background. The tunics of the figures are gilded with arabesques of red and green.
        After the period of Puritan persecution the chancel was ruinous in **1666** – this may have been the result of the destruction of the window glazing? William Le Neve from the College of Heralds visited many Norfolk Churches in 1630 and he recorded the armorial stained glass before its destruction during the 1640s. No record of a visit to Aylsham Church has yet been found.
Next to Bishop Jegon's large <u>memorial</u> on the north side of the chancel is a wall tablet to his son, John Jegon junior, **1621-31**.
The Jermy of Bayfield, and Wrench families intermarried; hence the presence of several Jermy memorials in Aylsham Church. Rev Jonathan Wrench, (1665-1740, 75); Rev Jonathan Wrench junior 1703-65. 62;
Mary daughter of Sir Benjamin Wrench, married John Jermy of Bayfield (he died in 1744); his third wife.

Missing from Aylsham Church; a <u>Royal Arms Board</u> of 1666.

12. '*The journal of William Dowsing (1596-1668, 72). Iconoclasm during the English Civil War'*,
        T. Cooper editor, 2001 pubn.
Dowsing was born in Laxfield, Suffolk into a family of small farmers. He moved to Codenham, in the centre of the county, married and had ten children. In 1640 he moved again, to the Stour Valley where Puritanism was rife. He was reacting against ecclesiastical authoritarianism – 'Bishops are a Babylonian love-token polluting the Lord's supper, misleading the promiscuous multitudes. Popish idolatry and corruption has brought religious tyranny. A new Reformation is needed. Evil must be confronted'. All this vitriol came from reading a large and eclectic collection of books mainly Calvinistic in leaning. Parliament's leader in the region was the Earl of Manchester who appointed Dowsing an officer and 'visitor'. He and his assistants reaped mayhem in the churches of the region – including Aylsham.
p363; **1641** he paid 1s-2d, to Christopher Tompson to take up the rails of <u>Aylsham Church</u>. Laudian altar rails were expensive to install in the 1630s. Perhaps Tompson and his assistants destroyed the stained glass and especially the armorial glass in Aylsham Church as nearly nothing remains now.

13. '*The early Art of Norfolk'*, Ann E. Nichols of West Michigan University, USA; 2002 pubn.
        Comments about Aylsham Church.
    1.   Three <u>Misericords</u> of 1470 are attached to a Victorian reredos (? – screen). The wooden carvings are
            similar to those found in Norwich Cathedral;
            A man with sword versus a dragon
            A bearded man with club versus hybrid monster
            A man versus griffin
            A man with protruding tongue

2. <u>Chancel Screen</u> carvings in wood;   standing angel with a . . .
   unicorn with eagle?   eagle standing on one leg
   bird with herbivore eating a flower seed pod   ox also on one hind leg
   carnivore eating snake   roaring lion with shaggy mane
   The items listed to the right were carved with animus and lively;   angel and lion (repaired)
   The elaborate gesso effects on the screen were expensive so the work was done piece-meal over a number of years.
   St Philip is shown holding a 'Tau' Cross – this shows a Continental influence in the artwork. Usually he holds a loaf of bread.
3. A Medieval wooden <u>roof boss</u> is carved with a wild man on it.
4. <u>Font</u>. Nicholas Pevsner thought the carvings had been much re-tooled during the Victorian restoration of 1852 but an older water-colour picture of the Font disproved that theory.
   Symbols of the Passion – a pillar of chords, two scourges, the Crucifixion etc. Relief on the bowl is 15thc also.
5. <u>Piscina</u> in the chancel. In the spandrel is a symbol of St Michael showing a late 13th century dedication.

Appendix (6) <u>Medieval documents related to Aylsham.</u>

1. <u>Post Mortem inquiries settling the estates of the deceased.</u>
1281, 9?Edward 1, v3; Reginald de Aylsham held ¼ knights fee in Swaffham Prior, Cambs.
1262, 46 Henry III, v1, #522; Richard de Whitwell, held 12 acres in Aylsham worth 33d paid yearly, & tallage paid to other sokemen.
1272, 56 Henry III; p810, Sheringham was held by the King for 12d service which was paid in Aylsham.
1280c, Edward I, v4; #315, Roger & Joan Aylsham his wife.
1336, 9 Edward III, v7, #683, p469; Sheringham was granted a market each Thursday by the King, as part of the Barony of Gifford for 8 knights fees, and 12d pa called '*war pud*', according to a deed by Richard I, given to Roger de Ludham and his wife Maud for her lifetime for £40 per year; and paid to the bailiffs of North Erpingham Hundred in Aylsham.
1280c, Edward I, v3, #464, p349; 24 acres in Aylsham were held from the king's ancient demesne, by John de Whitwell.
      same , #493, p 386; the same 24 acres were held in *socage*, doing a suit of court of the manor every three weeks for all (feudal services to the manor).
1315, 8 Edward II, vol 5, #116, p51, Sheringham was held for 1 knights fee and 12d/ paid yearly in Aylsham.
      same, #538, p332, the manor extent is given and there is a foreign view of frankpledge in Bru(n)dal.
Edward II, v6; , Edward III, v9, -
1354, 27 Edward III, v10, #82, p77; an inquisition held in Aylsham for the manor of Gresham.
1359, 32 Edward III, v10, #447, p356, 'in Aylsham there is a Saturday market, a fishery, an Xmas fair, 2 leets at St Peters in Chains festival and at Christmas. Queen Isabella holds it for life, service unknown'.
1364, 37 Edward III, v11, 489, p371; at an inquisition in Aylsham it was found that Alma was the wife of Sir Edward Burnel (Chancellor of England), deceased but her heir was unknown. She held manors in Norfolk in Riston and Thurning; and others in several other counties.
1372, 45 Edward III, v13, #117, p89; Inquisition for the estate of Sir Robert de Knollys on the Friday after the Day of Circumcision; some of the tenancies of Aylsham manor are held jointly but the service was unknown. The manor includes a moor, a <u>Saturday market</u>, a <u>Toll House</u>, an annual Christmas <u>Fair</u>, a <u>Leet</u> held on St Peter Chains Day each year.
1310c Edward II v13 blank; **1380**c Richard II, v15 & v16 blank,
Richard II, v 17; #292, In 'Aylsham-burgh' Christina wife of Geoffrey Alleyn of Crowend (Cromer) died in the previous year. She had a messuage in Aylsham off *inter-alia*, the Rev William de Tone/ Toune, chaplain of Aylsham by the king's license.
1400c, Henry IV, v18; 875, Christine, widow of Geoffrey Alleyns, of Cromer held East Beckham for a 1/8th knights-fee off *inter-alia*, William de Tone and had rents from Shipden (alias, Cromer). They died without children of their own. She died on 8 July **1392** and her estate was inherited by Cecily, daughter of Robert Aleyn, son of Roger Alleyn (her niece?).
1415c, Henry V, v20 blank, Henry VII, v21 blank.
1527, 18 Henry VII, 700, William Drake held a messuage called 'Mariots' in Brundale of Aylsham worth £4. Held from the Duchy Manor by fealty and 12d, paid yearly at Christmas.

2. Duchy of Lancaster records.

Sir William de Norwich, ally of the Duke of Lancaster was also his steward in the eastern counties (?)

    Ref; ' *Charters of the Duchy of Lancaster*' William Hardy, 1845; Norfolk Local Studies Library.

1313, Roger Bacon an adherent of the Duke of Lancaster was pardoned for a rebellion that started on Duchy land in Methwold.

1322, Duke of Lancaster's rebellion.

1371, the king gave special dispensation to the taxes paid by Flemish weavers and this caused offence to the Duke of Lancaster. He was appeased when in,

1372, a Charter was issued by Edward II to John Duke of Lancaster, King of Castille and Earl of Richmond which gave him extensive estates in Norfolk, including Aylsham; and in,

1377, the Hundreds of North Greenhoe, North & South Erpingham, Smithdon; and Aylsham, Wighton, Fakenham, Snettisham.

1381, 4 Richard II, Margaret Payn in Aylsham was appointed '*ancilla*' (servant of the manor) to the manorial workers (in the field?).

1381 during the Peasants' Revolt Richard II, was seen by some as conniving against his nephew the Duke of Lancaster by provoking the rebels in his Poll Tax.

1398, 21 Richard II; Hugh Fellow, was appointed as above, '*ad portandam ollam cum victualibus*' (to carry food in a pot (to harvesters?). He could be fined a substantial 2s-0d, if he did not perform this duty.

1399, Hundreds of Brothercross, North & South Erpingham, Gallow, also Methwold in the Duchy's control.

1459-60; Fakenham, Tunstead, Aylsham, Snettisham, Wighton, Gimingham and the Hundreds of paid fee-farm £28-6s-8d, in rent to the Receiver General who was also the Lord Treasurer of England.

3. Blickling records; Manuscript Commission report.

1. **1663** subsidy list for Aylsham, tax on land; the amounts levied on 22 people were fairly standard.

James	Allen,	20s,	8s, was paid in tax	Thomas	Lawes	20s	
Martha	Smith, widow	20s		Robert	Bur	40s,	10s, paid
Robert	Russell	40s		Anne	Britiffe, widow	20s	
Thomas	Brown	20s		Henry	Soame	20s	
William	Doughty	40s		Elizabeth	Brady	20s	
Francis	Curtis, guardian of;			Thomas	Barker	40s	
John	Brady	20s		Thomas	Leaman	20s	
Elizabeth	Lubbock, widow	20s		Rev Francis	Curtis	40s	
Richard	Curtis	40s		William	Wilson	20s	
Robert	Doughty gent	80s	32s, paid	Robert	Hall,	40s	
John	Durrant	40s		John	Ellis	20s	

Bailiffs & stewards of the Duchy in Aylsham.

1156, Henry II gave Aylsham to his brother William, Duke of Lancaster.

1199, it was granted to Eustace de Neville.

1226, granted to Hubert de Burgh.

1272, Edward I, held it for himself with Richard Cailly, bailiff.

1316, it was awarded to Sir David son of John Strathbogie, by the daughter of the Earl of Mar. He was taken a prisoner to England in 1300. On his return to Scotland in 1307 he rebelled against Robert the Bruce in Scotland and the returned to England when he was given by the English king three Norfolk manors including Aylsham. In 1322 he was called to the English parliament. In 1325 he commanded English troops in France and died in 1326. He was buried in Newcastle.

1330, granted Aylsham to Isabella dowager queen.

1399-1413, Sir Thomas Erpingham was gifted the Duchy Manor of Aylsham and he made Blickling Hall his main residence. Lord Baynard was later the steward of the manor.

1414, it was in the hands of the feoffers.

1459, Sir Edward Clere, of Blickling was bailiff for the Duchy and in,

1460, trustee for the will of Henry IV.

1546, Sir Arthur Hevingham, was sheriff etc, holding several other public offices.

1609, an inquiry was made in North Walsham into the ownership of the Duchy's estates in Aylsham.

1614, Sir Henry Hobart of Blickling was the bailiff.

1619, it was confirmed that James I, owned it so that king awarded it to the Prince of Wales who then became

Charles II, in 1625. He mortgaged it to the Corporation of the City of London except for the King's Mill in Aylsham.

1634, Sir John Hobart bought the Aylsham manor and served as deputy bailiff for the Duchy estates.

1636, Sir Edmund Barkham, bailiff.

1671 it was granted to the Earl of Sandwich. The gifting of royal estates was stopped by an Act of Parliament c1710. It reverted to the Hobarts, then Harbords, then Lothians, and in the late 1900s, to the National Trust.

1727, Duke of Rutland was chancellor of the Duchy estates, using the 'Duchy Chamber' in Westminster for Administration purposes.

1767, the Earl of Buckinghamshire, of Blickling, was the steward.p35. **1250**? Andrew de Brampton occupied 10 villanos (?), a messuage and 48 acres of land in the king's manor of Aylsham. Robert Cucuk had 10 acres and a messuage in the King's Manor by feofment and paid 3s-4d per year rent.

1320; 13 Edward II; Richard the newly appointed Vicar of Aylsham was a benefactor of St Peters College, Cambridge.

1389, 12 Richard II; the Vicar of Aylsham was threatened with distraint on his possessions for failing to make a payment for the accession of a new Lord of the Aylsham Lancaster Manor from whom he the Vicar held the a water-mill. The Vicar claimed exemption from payment due to a customary made in **1307** (35 Edward I) and a compromise was reached.

1601, there were already disputes over the rights on the Fir Ground of Aylsham's brewery – Abel Heath (see the survey map of this feature above) on the north boundary where the rights had to be 'adjusted' perhaps to stop the removal of peat and top-soil.

p81. **1616**, Lord Hobart of Blickling paid £80 per year for farming the Bailiwick of the Aylsham, Lancaster Manor from which were paid three officers; the coroner, ffeodary & escheator; and the market clerk.

1676; military items stored in the upper room of the church porch by order of the deputy Lord Lieutenants of Norfolk; 16 pick-axes, 5 wooden beetle; 4 hatchets, 24 mattocks, 23 spades, 100 yards of match, 2 bushels of musket shot, nearly a barrel full of gun-powder (what a threat to the church!)

1706, it was reported to a committee of deputy Lord Lieutenants of Norfolk, chaired by John Harbord of Gunton in response to an order in the Privy Council that there were Papists residing in Aylsham – Richard Parkes (recently deceased!) and a Mr Dickes.

4. *Feudal Aids*; manorial lordships;

vols 1 & 2, 1284-1431; blank.

vol 3, 1316, two manors recorded – those of the Abbey of Bury St Edmunds and the (Scottish) Earl of Athol.

5. Notes regarding the 'Calendar of memorandums rolls of the Exchequer';

1327; vol 3. 45; the sheriff of Norwich's advent leet with his attorney, Richard de Hindringham and others admitted Walter de Norwich to the manor of Aylsham for a rent of £40 per annum. He had paid £33 and ½ mark for Great Yarmouth, Ipswich, Burgh, Cawston, Aylsham, Fakenham which were all in the Queen's hands and various Hundreds assigned to John de Clavering.

same vol 2; nothing found;

Book of Fees part 2, also blank.

 same pt 3, 1236, an item of socage in Aylsham which is in the king's hands.

 p127, Hugh de Burgh, had been tenant of the king's demesne in Aylsham since King John's time.

Calendar of Genealogy, (Henry III – Edward I) nothing found.

Miscellaneous v4 and v6, blank.

 vol 3, 762; **1370**, a commission was held in Westminster enquiring into the estate of William Hestings, of Aylsham and other places. Administering the North and South Erpingham Hundreds was worth £30 per annum. Queen Phillipa had the service of the manor three years earlier but then the Sheriff could take the profits of the manor - £6, for writs and suits of prison; plus £3, for rents off various estates. The Duke (of Lancaster) held them by a royal charter. An inquest was then held in Norwich wanting a reply to the Sheriff's writ. Answer;

1346-7, 19/20 Edward III, it was farmed out by the Queen but to who?

6. Miscellaneous inquisition

Vol 2; 1307-10; **1337** The Mayor of London held an inquisition in the Tower of London.

He ordered Richard de Aylsham, the Bishop of London and several Earls to carry from London to Whitsend; worstead and woollen goods; bonnets, corones, pearls, some precious stones, etc and then to Calais, Bruges in Flanders, and Paris for the king's use.

Misc v1, blank.

Liberate Rolls Henry III, blank; Henry III, 1240-3, blank; 1245 - 1251, blank;

      v4, 262; for the keeper of the Aylsham Manor, a payment of £33-3-8d, to John le Breton in part payment of the yearly fee of £40 for justices, **1267-68**.

      v1,1234; blank; v2, Treaty Rolls, blank; Chancery 1277 - 1326, blank

Henry VII, Post Mortem v3, blank

7. Chancery Warrants, an enquiry was held at Langley by the lawyer, Walter de Norwich asking about tenants who had withdrawn their feudal services in Aylsham and Cawston. Sir John de Thorpe was appointed to investigate the case. He found that 40s was paid to Geoffrey de Aylsham the friar in the Order of Minors, for service and customs in **1309**, due since the king's mother Eleanor and *th . ise* . . (?)

1314, Geoffrey de Aylsham was recommended to become the new Bishop of Cloun in Munster, Ireland as 'he was a man of good life; honest talk and loyal to the king so it would be profitable for the government and church if he was so appointed'.

Richard III; letters & papers, foreign & domestic v21, pt 2; #332, p56 ?

8.   The Black Prince's Register, pt 4, 1351-65. Nothing found.

9.   State Papers, Domestic Foreign. Few entries relate to Aylsham.

1635, Robert Betts of Aylsham was called to the High Court in regard to his military commission but he failed to appear. A £50 bond issued against him was respited and in 1636 he seems to have renewed his commission.

10. Seven Mayors of Norwich who had links with Aylsham.

1. William Ashwell, MP five times 1433-45; Mayor **1441** & 1448, died in 1478. He was a merchant who left a widow Alice and children Henry, John, Catherine & Margaret. He owned property in Aylsham and left a bequest to the town.
2. Edward Cutler, Freeman in 1436, Sheriff 1453, MP 1460-61, Mayor **1470**. His widow Margaret married Richard Howard and they left a bequest for the south porch and sepulchre brasses in Aylsham Church.
3. Robert Portland, Freeman draper 1453, Sheriff 1464, Mayor **1477**, he and his wife Margaret were buried in Aylsham Church but their sepulchre brasses are lost.
4. Robert Jannys, Mayor in 1517 and **1524**. See notes above. His portrait hung in the Market Guildhall of Norwich and is the oldest civic portrait owned by the city. He was buried in St Georges Colegate in 1530. His PCC Will left a bequest to buy land for the benefit of Aylsham School.
5. William Rogers, a grocer in Brideswell Alley; Sheriff in 1531, Mayor in **1542** and 1548; also MP in 1542. He was buried in St Andrews Church, Norwich. He died sp in 1553 and left money to fund a school teacher in Aylsham's free grammar school.
6. Nicholas Norgate, mercer who owned the Maids Head Inn near Norwich Cathedral. He was the son of Alderman Thomas Norgate and had a brother also called Thomas Norgate. They had many relatives living in Aylsham. Nicholas was sheriff in 1553 and Mayor in **1564**. He married Agnes and had two daughters and died in 1568. He left his property in Aylsham and Blickling to fund a school in Aylsham.
7. John Wrench, Sheriff in 1669, Mayor in **1688**. He married Anne daughter of John Rayley who was Mayor in 1649; with issue John of Thwaite; Sir Benjamin Wrench MD; Jonathan Vicar of Aylsham from 1700 onwards.

Appendix (7) Ancient deeds.

1340, 13 Edward 3. 2761, to Sir John Fode of Aylsham; Sir John Froyset of Hocton; John de Haddiscoe chaplains; came into the ownership of land in Hevingham.

1342, 15 Edward 3, 2859, Sheep's Wong tillage etc, land in Hevingham sold to the same.

      2861, land in Irmingland was sold by them to the Prior of Mountjoy in Hevingland.

1344, 17 Edward 3, 2777; a sheep-fold was sold by John Shelton to the same people, Martin de Snitterlee, land in Hevingham.

1344, vol 5, 468; John Baghere of Heveringland senior; sold to John Fode, of Aylsham, who was rector of Irmingland; and John de Haddiscoe, chaplain; a land in Hevingham near a close; and two other lands in the same.

1350, 23 Edward 3; #2893, Roger de Heylwys of Irmingland to Sir John Fode, sold land in the same.

      23 Edward 3, #2821, Roger Heylewys, sold to the same chaplains more land in Irmingland.

1373, 46 Edward 3; #2891, yet more land in Hevingland near the common pasture was sold to the same chaplains.

1461, 39 Henry 6; vol 5, #10,942; John Holming of Marsham, sold to John Coppe (of Aylsham?), 8¾ acres of land in Matlaske.

1516, 7 Henry 8, #1,061; Goodman of Cawston sold to Henry Heydon esq, and Richard Pye of Erpingham, two messuages in Cawston, in Sygate, on *Boywood Field*; also Mowtings in Sygate, in *Wind Mill Field*. Vol . . there are several other references to the sale of lands in Hevingham at this time - #2759.

1538, 26 Henry 8; #12,162; a bond by Henry Winter of Winter Barningham, to Thomas Wode, of Aylsham yeoman, and others sold some land for £10, to be paid by All Hallows, with 100s deposit. These property transactions show how the manors of Aylsham became dispersed and extended into neighbouring parishes.

Appendix (8) Poll Taxes in Aylsham, 1377, 1379, 1381 etc.

Ref, '*Lincolnshire – Westmorland (including, Norfolk'*, Carolyn Fenwick editor; p144, 6199/12.

1377, 124 names listed, including 8 carpenters, 1 mason, 1 tailor, 1 black-smith, 3 text and 1 fabric workers.
1379 Tax Subsidy;

Aylsham		70 + people taxed		
Scottow	87 people listed,	58+	..	
Ingworth	47	..	..	35	..
Erpingham			47	..
Tuttingham			76	..
Blickling			77	..

1524, 15 Henry VIII; Subsidy Tax list for Aylsham.
   Volume 2, Walter Rye, Norfolk miscellaneous notes (NRO); p.403;

Edmund White,	£5 value	1s paid	Robert Northgate	£1	1s paid
Richard Croppe,	£40	40s paid	Margaret Wyme,	£1	1s
			Simon Skottow	£24	£4
			John James	£40	40s

1597, Subsidy Tax; ref Geoffrey Lowe, editor (PRO, E179/152/ 493).
In Aylsham, 44 (+ 1 who shared) paid tax on land; 15 paid for goods; 60 in total. Robert Wood's estate valued at £8; 32s paid (top of the list)
In South Erpingham, 6 paid £3+; 6 paid £4+; 9 paid £5+; 1 paid £15-19s. Total for the Hundred, 474 people paid (912 paid in 1522)
Sir Edward Clere, of Blickling Hall's estate valued at £30 - £6 paid.

Appendix (9) Crime in East Anglia in the 14th century

Traditionally every settlement in Norfolk had its stocks, pillory for whipping and a gibbet which was usually located in a dark corner of the parish, or at a cross-roads where it was more clearly visible. Reference has been found to a ducking stool. The stocks seem to have been in the Market Place.
1286, 14 Edward I; William Ponte of Aylsham accepted 8s-0d from William de Buere of Gunton and Clement the son of the Rector there, for removing them (illegally?) from jury service.
 1286; A person (unnamed) lodged with a couple, Ralph and Margaret. He murdered them in the night.
    There was a hue and cry after which he was caught; tried in Aylsham and hung.
Ref; *Norfolk Record Society* vol 44.
690; Reginald Stokes of Aylsham and eight others robbed Robert Pettit of 6s; Henry Woodhouse of 2s; John Long of North Walsham of 40d; Walter Rant of Woodbastwick of goods worth 5s; goods from Ranworth Mill worth 3s. They had no chattels. They placed themselves before the county for judgement and were hanged in Norwich; 4 August **1315**.
695; Simon and his brother, Reginald Siliby of Tuttington, robbed William Loning of Aylsham and others, of meat worth 18d; and Emma Brunt of Tuttington of silver worth 4s, and goods worth 3s. They had no chattels. They were hanged in **1316**.
492; Margery Bully and John of St Olaves (who died in prison) in Little Yarmouth stole 3 silver spoons worth 2s. Nicholas Siwhat under the pledge of John Lenen of Aylsham, the accuser, was not in court so his arrest was ordered. Margery was from Suffolk so she was entitled to a jury from there and was placed 'in mercy'.
441; John Danneys of St Olaves and Margaret Bully were arrested in Aylsham for burglarizing the above; 19 June **1315**.
273; William and his wife Cecilia Felix of Aylsham were arrested for the death of William Gryme of Hanworth who had been robbed of goods worth 40s, but they were acquitted, on a writ of *bono et malo*.
52. Thomas Atholf of Aylsham was accused of burglaring Martin Godfrey's house for goods worth 100s, and

some chattels. He was acquitted but John Robert was hanged for pilfering ½ Mark and 13 eels of black silk cloth; 7 August **1308**.

Appendix (10) <u>The textile industry and trade.</u>

Norfolk Archaeology vol 40, <u>Aylsham cloth</u> from 1301 onwards (the earliest reference found) was a prized commodity which was sent to Oxford at 1d/ 100 cloths; to Norwich Priory as a gift for vestments etc; for the royal household and the Great Wardrobe. It was extolled in romances. North-east Norfolk was the most densely populated part of England and it had a huge proportion of freemen. 1286, an agreement was made between Norwich and Picardy for the importation of dye stuff to supply the Norfolk textile industry.

Competition from high quality goods imported from Flanders, France etc harmed Norfolk's prosperity. Many weavers in Aylsham became mercers (traders) and gradually relocated to Norwich where the 'ulnager' was located (literal meaning; the inner bone of the arm, or inspector). Augustine de Aylsham for example was a linen draper who lived near St Peter Mancroft – the city's leading church. Workers in Aylsham had to economically diversify as partible inheritance reduced land holdings below the 10 acre subsistence level. Many became landless and turned away from farming to trades.

Aylsham Market.

1519, Richard Cross, Bailiff held a Saturday Market each week and an annual Fair on March 12th.

1705, Sir John Hobart bought the rights to hold a weekly market each Saturday charging for picage and stallage; and a Fair on Tuesday-Wednesday in September. A cattle fair was held each March 23rd and the last Saturday in September and October; but by 1906 these had lapsed.

29th May, Oak Apple Day was held to be an annual Club Holiday in Aylsham.

Appendix (11) <u>Aylsham in the 16th century.</u>

1524c, Muster in Aylsham; PRO Kew; E101.61.16
1584, Muster (27 Elizabeth 1), NRS vol 6, page 50
16 archers & 57 bill-men listed.

		selected persons		labourers & pyons	
Thomas	Bacon				
John	Brett	Thomas	Gay	John	Downing
Thomas	Larwood	Jeffrey	Burls	Thomas	Lubbock
John	Chestney	Robert	Menderby	Nicholas	Brett
Edmund	Green			Edmund	Scottow
John	Large	black-smith		Robert	Lubbock
Nicholas	Worstead	Lawrence	Pestall	John	Gogell
John	Cock (D) 17			John	Gay

17 men + one (too young?)
For the South Erpingham Hundred – endorsed by certificate in **1577**.
523 able-men; 292 furnished able-men; 10 trained able-men; 80 selected able-men, total;
Total (?) = 810 able-men + 231 unfurnished able-men + 180 pyons & labourers.
Captains & officers; Sir Christopher Heydon, Edward Clere, esq; Edward Paston, esq; John Dodge, esq.

<u>The Boleyn family and Blickling</u>. Sir Geoffrey Boleyn bought Blickling in 1459. His grandson Sir Thomas Boleyn, Earl of Wiltshire (he died in Hever Castle Kent in 1539) had a daughter, the future and ill-fated Queen Anne Boleyn (1501-36). She was born and may have been brought up in Blickling but at an early age was sent to be educated in the French court. In the later 1500s Blickling passed to the Clere family.

Appendix (12) <u>Some ancient street and place-names in Aylsham.</u> Ketton-Cremer mss, p6;

Sygathe Common'; between Erpingham & Aylsham, 13th c
'Hesland and . . . . . Ingworth Common pasture and woods' 4½ acres, in 2 pieces; 1298.
        Ate trane bush, Ingworth, 1319.
Back Lane became, Timber Lane; then in the late 1800s; Yaxley Lane was named after William Yaxley who lived at no 84, on the corner with Cawston Road as listed in the 1839 Tithe Map.
Sir William Lane, seems to have been named after Sir William Paston for whom it provided a short cut back from Aylsham to his home in Oxnead in the early 1600s.
Dyes Loke, named after Edward Dye who owned public houses in this part of Red Lion Street. There were eight dwellings leading off this alley running parallel to the south side of the churchyard.

Watery Lane, with 'Kirk Field' nearby. The name seems to have been changed to 'Dunkirk' in modern times.
Beck Hall, became Woodgate House. All the following six lanes and roads run in an east-west direction;
Coke's Lane, was renamed, Spa Lane; Reed Lane (further north) led eastwards into Stonegate.
Then came Cawston Road which has always had bends in it – perhaps to winde around areas of woodland.
Green Lane is further north; and Codlings Lane is even further north still. 'Hubbards Stye' leading to
Cawston – listed on an old survey of the parish boundary.
Brabons Lane, Heydon Road leads westwards to Abel Heath near the northern parish boundary.
Hend Beck flowed south through what is now Stourton Water (a lake) into Mermaids Beck.

MAP (31)

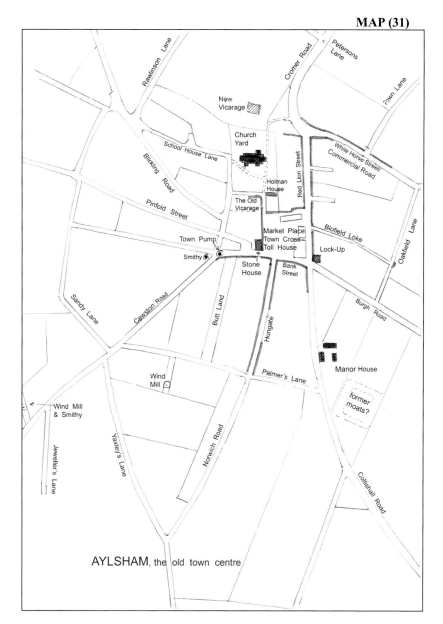

AYLSHAM, the old town centre

Other local place and road names;
Rodgate, Silvergate (in Blickling), Fengate, Frenclegate, Woodgate, Erpingham Sygate, Burgh Sponge
Causey. Also; Long Meadow, Jerbergs wood; Field names – Futters, Garoldstone, Raggard, Milbond, Turpets
Alder Carr, Starlings Hill, Stoke Croft, etc.
Besides the Great and Small Bridge of Aylsham there were others at Kettle, Bolwick/ Marsham, Brampton,
Burgh, Hok, Hom Reydyll.

Appendix (13) Aylsham in the 17th century

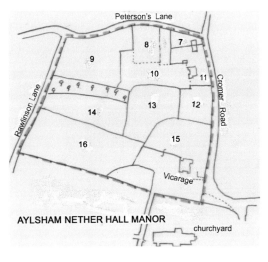

AYLSHAM NETHER HALL MANOR

1. The <u>four manors of Aylsham in the 17th c</u> –
   a/ <u>Lancaster Manor</u> since 1156, by Edward III.
   b/ <u>Wood Manor</u> so named when Henry VIII, gave it to Edward Wood.
   c/ <u>Bolwick</u> the smallest manor, 1153-68; there were no tofts there.
   d/ The <u>Vicarage Manor</u> was given to Battle Abbey and later to the Dean & Chapter of Canterbury; when it extended into several adjacent parishes. Map 32 (left) shows the Aylsham Nether Hall Manor (and the possible former extent of the Vicar's Manor) with owners listed in the 1839 Tithe Assessment Schedule (NRO).

MAP (32)

2, <u>The Lord Lieutenant of Norfolk's journal</u> NRS (*Norfolk Record Society*), vol 45;
1666, 3.7; (page 90); Sir John Holland's regiment rendezvoued at Aylsham.
1670, 12.7; (page 117) Mr Gregory of Aylsham was the Collector for the same, £1-5s-11½d.
(page 64); the South Erpingham collection;

Aysham	£17-3s-10d/ month,	£4-5s-11d/ week
Blickling	£6-5s-6d	£1-11s-4d
Erpingham	£4-15s-0d	£1- 3s-5d
Hundred total	£83-8s-6d	£20-16s-0d

3, <u>Muster records</u>
1673, South Erpingham defaulters for the militia muster at Heydon Ollands; Robert John & William Brady of Aylsham? refused to find arms. Robert Russell the same who had defaulted for three years. Fined 20s.

4, James son of <u>William Reymes</u> of Overstrand (LOM) was baptised in Aylsham, in 1578.
William Payne married Anne Reymes in Aylsham. John Reymes lived in Aylsham in the early 17th c.
Robert Reymes of Aylsham born in 1535, was the son of John Reymes of Suffield. Col Reymes was a dominant and ruthless agent for Parliament in the district during the 1640s.

5 'The Tofts of Aylsham Lancaster Manor', a survey made in1624;
   Norfolk Archaeology, 1995, p42; 148-159; by Joan Turville-Petre. The term is Scandinavian, meaning a land-holding. Its use was extended into Aylsham.The total area of tofts etc listed in the survey add up to –
2443¾ acres in total plus many small ¼ - ¾ acre plots.   See the abbreviated schedule below.
   NA, 1995; 148 – 159; *'The Tofts of Aylsham'*.
Aylsham Lancaster, a roll of 1462, showed 62 tofts. This number was quickly reduced.

Aylsham Wood Manor,	44 tofts
Aylsham Vicarage Manor,	9 tofts
Aylsham Bolwick Manor	none

Each toft was represented by a manorial officer such as '*messor*', or Hayward/ collector; '*ballious*' was a lower office; eg Elston Toft, near Holloak Mere in Aylsham Woods and near the Banningham boundary. Tofts remained in use into the 16th century in the Aylsham Wood and the Aylsham Vicarage Manors because they were ecclesiastical with more continuity and more conservative in their management than in the Aylsham Lancaster Manor.

   In the 17th century, much of the wild-life was considered 'vermin' and persecuted, sometimes to extinction. This included weasels, stoats (called 'lobsters'), pole-cats, hedge hogs, rats, mice, badger, birds nesting on the church etc.

6, NRS vol 15, 154; '<u>*Lord Lieutenant's Journal'*</u>. The County jury was made up of Norfolk's gentry who acted as local magistrates, tax collectors and occasionally came together in the Shire Hall next to Norwich

Castle to judge prisoners held in the squalid dungeons of the Castle.

c1630; Walter Wright had a wife and two children living in Aylsham. The jury ordered that he was to remain in the Norwich Bridewell until he agreed to leave the city and return to them.

p95; Thomas Blofield was born in Aylsham but was found to be a vagrant (and begging?) in Norwich. He was punished and sent back to Aylsham with a pass.

Robert Searle of Aylsham was convented before the Mayor of Norwich. He sold 10 combs of wheat to baker for a down payment of 12d which was to be sold in the market.

7. NRS vol 14, When Sir Henry Hobart, chancellor to the Prince of Wales was granted the manor of Aylsham and its appurtenances with other places for 23 years, in 1625 he settled it on his daughter Philippa Hobart.

8. NRS vol 44, '*The papers of Nathaniel Bacon of Stiffkey, Norfolk 1599- 16..*', 2000pbn.
p86; in **1599**, Bacon was the High Steward in Norfolk for the Duchy of Lancaster.
Bick Stockdale, servant of the Duchy's under-steward Robert Godfrey; lodged a case against John Elger & Edmund Smith of Sedgefield at the Duchy Court (in Aylsham?).
p228; **1602**, the liberties of the Duchy to claim for 'wreck and groundage of goods' (dumped by a storm on the north Norfolk beaches) were often impeached (ie challenged) by the Admiralty's agents. Information to this effect was presented to the Duchy Chamber, in the Palace of Westminster. An Admiralty Court was held in what is now the Red Lion pub in Cromer each winter to resolve competing claims.
p4, **1603**, Sir Henry Sidney was the Duchy's receiver in Eastern England.
    1604, Christopher Reeve was deputy to Richard Bunting, bailiff of Gallow & Brothercross Hundreds

9. NA vol 45, pt IV; p 468,
1597 Sir Henry Hobart bought the Acle estate off his relative Thomas Clere. This was his first step towards enlarging his holdings.
1602, Elizabeth I, granted two other Norfolk manors to Sir Henry Hobart.
1606, his daughter Dorothy married Sir Robert Crane, the nephew of Lady Agnes Clere.
1610, the Crown granted him Marsham, Cawston and Hevingham Park.
1616, Lady Agnes sold Blickling to Sir Henry.
1622 the King granted a lease on the Duchy estates in Aylsham to Sir Henry.
1623 Sir Henry purchased the remainder of the Clere estates in Weybourne and Wymondham to him. Sir John the son of Sir Henry Hobart later bought the Lancaster estates in Aylsham after a long struggle with the Aylsham tenants. This completed the formation of the Blickling estates in just 26 years.

10. **1601-09**, Nicholas Easton was a teacher in Aylsham School and he helped several boys to enter Cambridge University (NRS).

11. Civil War period and the Church.
1654, E. Bulwer, conducted marriages in secular ceremonies in Aylsham. Probably Sir Henry Hobart and
    Thomas Toft, Mayor of Norwich did the same in the town. So did William Steward.
Sir John Hobart and Robert Doughty were the impropriators of the tithed corn for the west and south sides of the parish at that time.

12. '*Civil War and Norfolk*', by Robert Windham Ketton-Cremer. Entries related to Aylsham;
    Page 18; John Jegon was the Bishop of Norwich in the years of James I. As an unpopular Master of Corpus Christi College in Cambridge he was a disciplinarian and was often satyricised for it. He knew his clergy well but did not make excessive demands for conformity even from Puritan preachers. He had a wife much younger than himself and was parsimonious with her. He gave little to charity or exercised hospitality just to gain promotion for his children. He saved money by living in the clergy house of Ludham instead of his palace in Norwich. The former house burnt down in 1614 so he moved to his own house in Aylsham living there for four years before his death in 1618. Sir Charles Cornwallis of Beeston married Jegon's widow. Cornwallis had been the Treasurer to the Prince of Wales. Jegon's son Robert built a house for himself in Buxton and was in trouble over his sympathies for the royalist cause in the 1640s.

    Page 51; several Norfolk MPs met in Aylsham, Holt and Walsingham on 8 October **1641,** to collect subscriptions in support of Parliament's struggle in the civil war. They were accompanied by five to eight magistrates and Deputy Lord Lieutenants. The pretext for the collection was to oppose the invasion of Norfolk by foreign troops especially by those raised in Holland by Charles I's queen. The MPs had been given several Hundreds to manage collectively. They also met in Yarmouth, Lynn, Norwich and Thetford. They carried silver plate to the meetings which represented the main valuables owned by the gentry. Sir John Potts of Mannington gave 2 horses, 10 guns and £100. Sir John Palgrave gave a similar amount. At the second meeting Sir William Paston (a well known royalist) offered £200, plate and 6 horses but only for the defence of Norfolk. The rest of the valuables were sent down to London.

p190; in April **1643** there was a disturbance in Aylsham with a parade and demonstration in the market place. It was a protest against the payments levied on them by the Norfolk county committee for the war. A trained band of soldiers rode swiftly up from Norwich and managed to nip the rising in the bud before bloodshed was spilt. The ring leaders were arrested. Later they received an order to prepare a certificate showing the value of their estates and to present it to the 'Committee of Compounding' in the Goldsmiths Hall in London. Several members of the minor gentry from Aylsham were fined for delinquency between a tenth to a third of their estates.

p301; Thomas Leman, attorney of Aylsham was fined £367; Edward Colfer, another attorney of Aylsham, £940, but the fine was reduced to £320; Robert Burgh £407, reduced to £370 as he had a wife and ten children. Richard Curtis of Aylsham and Richard Allen of Tuttington were each fined £20. Colfer was later engaged in the king's cause and went to Oxford to serve him. Some clergy also actively supported the 'tumult' including the rector of Alby and Sustead.

p204; the Rev Richard Howes, rector of Knapton was ejected from his living and later gaoled in the Aylsham lock-up. One of the other inmates was the dangerous Thomas Turner. Howes later petitioned for Turner to be removed to Norwich Prison in the castle. Many other clergy in the district were ejected.

p251, Rev Nathaniel Gill son of the headmaster of St Paul's School in London was a witty classicist. He was rector of Burgh 1638-44 when he was ejected from the living by the Earl of Manchester's order. He remained in the village and continued to serve the parish in secret with the support of his church-wardens until 1651 when he was made to leave for Bungay. In 1660 he triumphantly returned to Burgh with the church register which he had kept so that no imposter could use it. Between 1663 and 1669 he was vicar of Aylsham but he died after that and was buried in Burgh.

Appendix (14) A few 18th century records relating to Aylsham

1. Poll Books of voter in Aylsham,
     1714, 5 names - Jonathan Wrench, clerk; who published '*The principle duties of the Christian Religion*',
        See their family ledger slab memorials in the Sanctuary of Aylsham Church.
     1700. James Lubbock, Benjamin Woolsey, Mil Baspoole, Thomas Carr.
        1768, 18 names; 1802, 24 names including John Warnes.
2. Daniel Defoe the writer visited Aysham in 1732.

3 Aylsham Road Orders. Their enrolment, registration & deposit.
    1. NRO, C/Sce 2/28/1, box 28, **1796**; a footpath was stopped up where it crossed 'Further Doctor's Pightle' and replaced by a new path along the public highway.
    2. NRO, Box 1, no 18; Book 8, 260-266? A highway to Millgate, diverted, 9.8.**1777**
    3. NRO, Book 5, p223-4, 'A footpath diverted' with a plan; 10.2.**1798**.
    4. Book 28, 1-; City Hall legal services department.

4. In **1722**, Sir John Hobart gave land to Aylsham measuring 14 x 15 yards, part of the Ollands in the Bridewell for use as a common watering place. Until then occupants of dwellings needed a legal right to access a well to supply domestic water. NRO FX 232/1

5. The writings of Robert Windham Ketton-Cremer of Felbrigg.

1. '*Country Neighbourhood*' – the letters of the Rev Patrick St Clare, rector of Sustead written to his patron William Windham of Felbrigg Hall, Norfolk. He was a Scot called Sinclair who disguised his birth name by Anglicising it to 'St Clare'.

p31; Aylsham was one of thirty market towns in Norfolk which were the busy centres of local life and sometimes cut off from the rest of the county. In winter this could bring local hardship when essential supplies could not reach the town or trade goods sent to market.

p72; 13.7.1732; Sinclair suspected that letters coming from Aylsham are often opened and read perhaps by people looking for the politically and religiously disaffected.

p89; 30.9.1732; Mr Scott of Aylsham wrote to Lord Hobart of Blickling that Mr Gay of Calthorpe had a pack of hounds which would probably trespass on his lordship's estate. Gay was ordered to keep out.

p103; 12.4.1733; only two men living in Aylsham voted Tory in the election of that year which saw a Whig victory.

p117; 24.9.1736; the Rev Jonathan Wrench junior had been the rector of Metton until 1733 when he took over Aylsham from his father, Jonathan Wrench senior. His father by exchange took over Metton but then he became too ill to stay in post so the arrangement was reversed. His grand-children remained at school in Aylsham. Young Mr Wrench was advised that holding two livings in plurality was unacceptable. He also liked to go hunting until he was strongly advised against it by Colonel Harbord Cropley Harbord of Gunton.

p150; 15.6.1738, the mineral spa was fashionable amongst the lesser gentry of Aylsham who liked to drink the waters for their health. (The Spa was used mainly for asthma suffers and others with chest infections)

p171; 14.9.1738; the young Rev Tayleure, rector of Gunton was living as a boarder in Aylsham with a widow Mrs Athill and her young daughter. Tayleure was often seen with the girl in public which caused gossip.

p179; 5.10.1738; Lord Hobart had recently extended Blickling Park, eastwards towards Aylsham. This was to accommodate a garden mound, plantations, geometric walks and a temple (now owned by the National Trust). Mr Gallant of Aylsham had recently sued the Rev(?) Whitacre for a loan he had made. By then Mr and Mrs Wrench had moved to a house in Aldborough (a village north of Aylsham).

p206; 12.2.1739; the Rev Tayleure had married Miss Athill even though the girl was poor and in weak health. The paternalistic Col Harbord of Gunton had advised Wrench against the marriage. When the Rev Sinclair went to Aylsham to wish them well he found the couple had already left for Norwich where a marriage settlement was to be drawn up. Tayleure had a wealthy uncle who was to give each of Mrs Athill's other children £100 each. These notes give some idea of the social intercourse between the gentry.

2, 'Norfolk Assembly', by Ketton-Cremer.

p30; repeat of p51 above.

p115; Aylsham is charming to us in the modern age but to previous visitors it was only 'neat and clean'. This was in contrast to North Walsham where waste water ran down the middle of the main streets and next to the town pump. Lady Beauchamp-Procter of Langley Hall, Norfolk visited the town in 1764 and 1772. She wrote that two undertakers in the market square (?) of Aylsham lived opposite to each other. The charges of the Blackboys Inn were reasonable. She was unimpressed with Blickling with its 'old fashioned' architecture and lack of old trees in the park.

3, 'Norfolk Portraits', by the same.

11.4, p164; Lord Walpole of Wolterton Hall raised a troop from men in and around Aylsham in 1803 when there was a severe threat of invasion by the French.

Appendix (15) Aylsham in the 19th century.

1 The canalised River Bure.

Wherries could weigh up to 13 tons fully loaded. If they weighed more they could exceed the 2½ feet draught in the canal which was only 3 feet deep after dredging. One wherry got stuck in the mud after the 1912 great flood and had to be broken up. Wherry men resorted to using a 'quaint' or, punting pole if there was no wind. The sails were painted with black tar. There were 26 wherries at one time – one of them was converted to carrying passengers to Great Yarmouth. Records show that 7,500 tons of cargo (only) passed through the locks but up to 30,000 tons were thought to have been carried each year. After the closure of the canal a wherry was taken to France and used as a pleasure boat. Very few of the large number of wherries that once existed survive today.

A Steam Mill using coal for fuel, was built in 1856. It was converted to diesel in 1929 and closed in 1979. Mills were used for grinding corn, pumping ground water, pummelling cloth, cutting wood, driving machinery.

2, **1822**, Mr Bartram of Aylsham fitted up a clock on buildings at Haveringham Hall.

He was engaged in one of the skilled trades of the town.

3, **1851**, there were five thatchers living in Aylsham district.

4. The cost of property and development.

Town Hall, cost £2100; Canalisation of the River Bure cost £6,010; the School in 1848, cost £700. It was enlarged in 1875. In the early 1700s it only had 6 boy pupils and one school master.

The Workhouse, with 12 acres of land and built for 619 inmates costing £12,000 but it only held 130 inmates in 1906. Land for a new cemetery in 1885, cost £600.

Appendix (16) Maps of Aylsham and district.

1580, a map of the complete parish of Cawston; NRO/ NRS 21399 C/ SCfl list;
  copied from Cambridge University Library; a 16th c map of common heath and severals between Cawston
  & Aylsham.
1624 rental list for Aylsham, with 109 tenants including 20 women. PRO E315/ 360.
1622, Fx11
1729, a modern tracing of a survey map displayed by the National Trust inside Blickling Hall and surveyed by
  James Corbridge.
1772, Henry Biedermann's survey for the canalisation of the River Bure – Aylsham Town Council archive
  department.
1814, Enclosure map NRO, C/ Sca/ 261 – Burgh by Aylsham showing shared river frontage.
1816, Estate of James Bulwer of Aylsham Manor House; NRO, BR 276/1/ 0941
1840; Tithe survey and schedule of Aylsham; made 1 August 1839 by James Wright.
1885; Ordnance Survey map at a scale of 6" to the mile – the earliest.

Appendix (17) Historic images of Aylsham.

1 The Rev James Bulwer painted a views of;
      a/ the northern end of Norwich Road c1830? with Bank House on the right and two gabled houses left,
one in the distance near the Market Place. The original is in the Norwich Castle Museum collection.
      b/ Aylsham Bridge and Inn.
2. The 'Buttlands', was originally 220 yards long, between Cawston and Mill Roads; (see image above) now
  170 yards. 1363, Edward III, required archery practice on Sundays and holidays. Sir Thomas de Erpingham
  took his local men with their long bows and he led them at the Battle of Agincourt.
3. Photograph of the John Soame Memorial (Town) Pump was given a thatched canopy. This was rethatched
  in 2014. The town's wells were not replaced by a public water supply until 1938.
4. Photograph of one of the last stage-coaches parked outside the Black Boys Hotel in the late 1800s. It
  travelled between Cromer and Norwich via Aylsham.
5. Market Day was on a Monday and Saturday with a farmers' market on the first Saturday each month.
6. From the late 1600s onwards old buildings were given a make-over by adding a brick façade to their
  frontages. This provided an opportunity to use a new and fashionable design but the practical reason was to
  reduce fire risk. A few houses retained their external timber frame and thatched roof.
7. There are several yards and pightles in Aylsham; Peggs Yard, off Red Lion Street; Dykes Loke, off the
  Market Place; Blofield Loke off the east side; Rookery Yard off Hungate Street;

Appendix (18) Buildings of Aylsham with statutory listing as of historical of value.

Parish Church, grade 1. 50m east-west, by 34m north-south; tower 30m high to the battlements.

Aylsham Old Hall, Blickling Road; - grade 1 (All other listed buildings in Aylsham noted below, are grade II).
A portrait of the house was painted soon after the Old Hall was completed and placed in an over-mantel in the
main upstairs chamber. A large brick barn can be seen in the picture on the left of the house. Between it and
the house is a partly walled garden with a central fountain. This and the forecourt were laid out in a formal
Dutch style. The central entrance door to the house looks westwards down a tree-lined avenue. Blickling Road
runs across the picture between house and avenue. To the right is an ornamental canal and to the left, a statue
on a plinth (see the image above).

1 Burgh Road, 18thc with a hipped roof and smut pantiles, 2 storeys, brick pilasters.
Anchor Inn, once a house but licensed in 1781 as a pub. This lies next to the Malt House on the west side of
Millgate.
Abbot's Hall; early 18thc, red brick, hipped pantiled roof, 2½ storeys high with sash windows.
Abbot's Hall Barn, 75 metres to the west of the above but separately listed It has early 18thc brick and a
      thatched roof.
Abbots Hall Farm House. Early 17thc but much altered. Steep, plain and pantiled roof; modern casements;
      stone quoins and brick diaper patterns; a brick & flint plinth.
Bayfield House, commanding the view at the northern end of Red Lion Street. 1750 – it has a fine staircase.
The Beeches, 54 Holman Road; 18thc and built over an earlier core. Brick and colour wash; steep pantiled

roof, 2½ storey; casements in the rear.

The Belt, home of the milling family of Parmenter. It has a tall, north facing Dutch gable with the tie-iron letters '1741, TRE' attached to it. It was much enlarged in a classical manner in the 1820s. Tannery once attached to it. The Thatched Lodge on the corner of Sir William Drive is where the drive to the house begins.

Church Hill House, 18thc, brick & flint walls, a hip on the west side.

The Corn Hall was built in the Market Place in 1857. Later it became the Town Hall, with a magistrate's court house; a large assembly room with offices above; the Town's Archives; cellars. The western extension replaced London House. That Georgian house had an elegant bow-front but no garden or yard as a passage lay behind it.

12 & 14 Cromer Road, Parmenters & Clyde Cottage; 17thc and later; brick & flint, shaped gables, sashed windows etc.

Dell Farmhouse. Brick & stucco walls; symmetrical front, pantiled roof, sashes & architraves, 2 brick stacks.

Diggens Farm House, Buxton Road; red brick, steep roof with pantiles, modillioned eaves, shaped gable north.

Hill House and garden wall south & west, Heydon Road. 2 storey L-shaped plan, pedimented doorway; casement windows.

Holman House, on the south side of the Church-Yard. Built in 1760, it faces north with a sash window either side of an elegant central doorway. There is also a western entrance leading to a fine sweeping staircase. Beneath the west side of the house is an under-croft measuring 7.63 x 3.3 metres with brick vaulting 3m high, supported by five slightly pointed and chamfered brick arches (14th c?). Brick and flint walls with 11 small lantern niches and one big one. The original entrance was probably from the south. The cellar is aligned north-south, parallel to the adjacent path. The house has a small southern extension of 1820 with a charming Regency balcony. The under-croft runs below the 1760 house and its 1820 extension. Thomas Cooke was one of its owners. A pipe trench was dug adjacent to the house and the Churchyard gate in 1955. A four feet thick, wall foundation was discovered but not dated – did it relate to an earlier house or a pre-Medieval building?

Manor Farmhouse, Heydon Road, 17thc red brick, steep pitched roof, pantiles, a T-shaped plan; crow gable and shaped gable north with internal stack. Wooden portico with fluted columns.

Malt House, in Millgate. On the wall, 'R. Parmenter 1781'. A long building with its east gable facing the road. This is a rare survivor of its type.

IMAGE (30)

The Manor House (left). The medieval house was probably where the ponds are east of the house – was it originally moated? The present building lies further west and it dates from c1580. It lies on an east-west axis with a central dining-hall. This room has the longest moulded beam in Norfolk. It has a roll and concave chamfers. The room also has moulded cornice beams. In 1610 Bishop Jegon updated the house. The main façade was again remodelled with sash windows in 1680. A western extension may date from then - the plan narrows on this side of the house. The cellars are under that part. The elaborate staircase with twisted balusters is Georgian. It opens off the south side of the Hall. In 1880, ancillary buildings and wings were added at the rear south side. The building is now a care home.

Unicorn Pub; Hungate Street. 17thc with a steep roof; L-plan, Stacks in the gables. Originally it was thatched but later given a pantiled roof; L-plan, 2 storeys, small windows. On the old bowling green a marquee was erected for the 'Cinematographic Palace', Aylsham's first and only cinema; 1914-21.

(The three) Black Boys Inn, was first recorded in 1659. A passage to the rear stables went through the middle of the building with bar-rooms either side and the ballroom – assembly room extends over all three parts. The ground floor northern room has a high ceiling with heavy moulded beams. There is a Jacobean staircase with turned balusters. The Inn is on the western side of the Market Place.

1 Market Place (south side) see notes below on the Repton family. John Repton died in 1775 aged 61 and he left it to his children. Later, Robert Copeman and his sons moved from 1 Norwich Road (opposite) and took over 1 Market Place. South side of the Market Place, which was previously, Gurney's Bank.

8-9 Market Place, late 18thc, red brick, modern shops frontages below; sash windows with keystones.

10 Market Place, Rendered colour wash, 2½ storey, wooden eaves, shop front, 18th c.

11. Also 18thc with a shop front 2½ storeys, grey pantiles.

12 & 13, mid 18thc with grey pantiled roof.

14. late 18thc entry doorway with an entablature.

15. steep pantiled roof, 2½ storeys plus cellars. This was Dye's House in the early 1800s. It later became an office for solicitors, and others.

16. A modern restaurant, early 19thc, included for group value. Brick & colour-wash; steep roof.
17. 19thc with a hipped roof, 2 storeys. The former Cocglan Chemists displayed a chemist's pot above the elegant shop front, which is still there.

IMAGE (31)   **IMAGE (32)**

21. International Stores – now (2014) the Cooperative Store, on the north side of the square. Mid 18thc with later changes.
 30. Market Place, south side; 18thc, 3 storeys; pantiled roof, keystones over the windows, painted, corner pilasters.
Hungate Street; nos 12, 14, 16, 18, 24, 28, 30, 32, 34, 36, 38, 40 (with a 17thc core), 46, 48, 50, 64
                    9, 11 (later with shops), 13, 21 (with a moulded timber beam), 23, 29 (dated 1763), 33, 35, the rest are 19 thc; 37, 39, 43, 47, 51Gothic House, with white walls it has two blank windows facing the street.
        29 houses on this street are 'listed'!
13 Hungate Street, Norfolk House has a very classical design with a porticoed front door.
40 Hungate Street, a long thatched house – perhaps originally several dwellings.

Harvest Moon Cottage, with a 2 storey workshop behind with wooden boarding.
35 Hungate Street; a 17th c, cottage with timber framed walls face the street.
White House, and White House Cottage; late 17thc, and later, pantiled and slate roof, hipped, attic casements with leaded lights.
IMAGE (33) Woodgate House.
Woodgate House, (left) was started in 1706, and only completed in 1726 (the date is over the entrance door). It was built on the site of an earlier house. Built for the Soame family, it was occupied by a Judge, Arthur Boulderson who died there in 1915. It is a fine building with a hipped roof of smut pantiles; gabled dormer windows, moulded modillions, brick pilasters. The drawing room has a fine Georgian mantelpiece. A later north wing was added with a shaped gable. The garden walls have rusticated piers.

The Old Vicarage; built in 1700 but much altered in the 19thc. Brick dentilled eaves, flat roofed dormers,
        2½ storeys, old panelling inside. Testimony – Mr Thexton (son of the parson?) was a shop-keeper, related to the Barker family of whom there were many members in Aylsham.

The Bridewell. Inside there was a beam measuring 37' by 10" wide and inscribed 'to Robert & Joan Marsham, by whom this building was made (etc) 1543', with their Shield of Arms and initials RM/ JB.
A curious pair of barbarous instruments was found there used for catching a fleeing offender by the legs. They were in the shape of a long pitch-fork with a spring web 7' – 8' long called a 'catching tool'.

2, The Mills of Aylsham
    1. The great King's Water Mill was bought by the Parmenter family in 1798. They already owned the adjacent Malt House since 1777. By the late 1800s they had been taken over by John and Stanley Bullock as millers. Occupants of the Kings Water Mill;   1370, Edward III granted it to Sir Robert & Constance Knollys.

104

IMAGE (34) Aylsham Mill

1648, Capt Doughty, paid £60/pa in rent + a fee farm of £18-6s-8d.

1670, William Purdy

167? William Thory held it for a year

1675-78, Bartholomew Willis.

1680, Robert Sexton who was charged tithes of £3 per annum but objected.

1683, Miles Baspoole bought it for £3,750 and the School claimed £10 per year from him.

1696-99, William Smith paid only £30 rent but it was in poor repair by then.

1700s, Thomas Spurrell ran the mill with Joseph Ames and Thomas Harvey, mill-wright of Aylsham. Spurrell died in 1770.

1771, Robert Parmenter bought the mill and he rebuilt it – his initials are on a date stone on the building. This anticipated the Bure Navigation Act of 1773. The mill had four floors; two water wheels and five pairs of grinding wheels.

1851, the census shows Samuel Parmenter aged 51 as the miller, corn merchant & malster. He ran the mill with Bullock (who later bought it off him), 8 journey-men millers and a master miller. Parmenter died in 1872 in Morden College, Blackheath.

1864, the Bullock brothers owned it. Stanley Bullock died in 1914.

IMAGE (35)

1937, Ben Rust was the last miller. The machinery was still in place after 2001.

2005, the former Granary in the southern wing was converted into four flats.

2. The Vicar's Water Mill is shown on the 1729 Survey Map of Blickling by James Corbridge. It lay a short distance north of the town bridges. There are currently 17 dwellings on that road leading to Abbot's Hall.

3. One Windmill stood behind no 5, Mill Road off the Cawston Road. It was built in 1826 for Henry Soame. It closed in 1895 and it was damaged by lightening in 1900. The cap and sails blew off in a gale in 1920 but the tower is still there. Another windmill stood on the south side of the town.

4. 1864, a Steam Mill opened in Dunkirk to rival the water and wind mills.

IMAGE (36) (ref; Martyn Gregory, art dealer)

3. Aylsham's Bridges.

1759, the southern wooden bridge over the River Bure was rebuilt in brick by mason William Berry.

1821, the bridge over the Bure Navigation Canal was also rebuilt in brick by Mr Berry (son of the above?). Both these bridges had been in existence for a long time by then. They both survived damage from the massive 1912 flood mainly because water from the river managed to escape around them by Mash's Row.

In the painting left made by Thomas Lound (he died in 1861) are shown the brick abutments of the bridge; a thatched cottage (now gone) and the Dutch gable of the Anchor Inn. Further right is the church tower and steeple.

Appendix (19) <u>Some of the Public Houses of Aylsham in the 19th century.</u>

1. <u>Black Boys Inn</u>, a messuage with a cottage ('The Stone House') in 1471. 1588 Rachel Norgate, was the owner with 20 Perches of land. It had an assembly room, 10 bedrooms, 2 attic bedrooms for maids; a rear kitchen, bar, external larder, cellar, tap room, Justice Room, Commercial room, wash house, a post lads room. It was part of the Aylsham Lancaster Manor. Only its Jacobean staircase survives inside. The central door facing the Market Place was once an entrance to a passage-way leading to the rear stables for the horses. Ref; *'The Black Boys Inn and the Aylsham Wood Manor'*, S. Rowland, 1979 pubn - a leaflet.
'Black Boys' is a term thought to derive from the nick-name of Charles II but it was once called the 'three' black-boys. Another explanation is that the name may be an Anglicisation of 'Black Bois' as in the Black Forest of Germany, a name in circulation in the 17thc.
2. <u>Unicorn Inn</u>, Hungate Street; a 30' long cellar, an L-shaped layout plan, bowling green left of entrance. It was built in the 17thc, with a half-timbered frame.
3. <u>Half Moon</u>, 19 Hungate Street; with a brew and bake house there before 1700.
4. <u>Swan</u>; recorded before 1620; it lies further south along Hungate Street. Robert Beasey owned it in 1837. Adjacent to the pub was Beasey's 'Rookery' where he built 13 modest cottages.
5. <u>Dog</u>; Norwich Road, Aylsham Lancaster Manor land; Thomas Allen owner in 1689; a 5 bedroom house 28' frontage; 6 stables behind and a coach-house; a court room 34' frontage 2t5' deep; pub between them.
6. <u>Angel</u>, on the corner of Burgh & Norwich Roads. In 1615 it had 2½ acres of land attached and a further Ollands/ Angel Close of 11 acres. Thomas Cressey was the owner in 1615 (see above).
7. <u>New Inn</u>, 10 Red Lion Street, with Blofield Loke down one side. This yard had stables in it. The property stood on the north side of the Bull Inn. It was called the 'Kings Head' until 1791. It was built on the site of a medieval structure and rebuilt again in 1689, but still with a half-timbered frame.
8. <u>Bull Inn</u>. This was a small thatched building up to 1907 when its use changed to a fish-monger and later to a garage work-shop. This and the New Inn were demolished about 2003 and replaced by modern shops sympathetic to their setting. See notes above of the archaeological finds made on the site.
In the 1841 census, 159 people lived on the west side of Red Lion Street, and 92 on the east side; a total of 249 people out of Aylsham's total population of 2448 (ie about 10%).
9. <u>King's Head</u>, Red Lion Street; a half-timbered building of 1689 or earlier. Its yard stretched back to Oakfield Road to the east. It had 8 bedrooms and a bowling green where a tented theatre was erected in the 19thc. It closed in 1953.
10. <u>Red Lion</u> on the opposite west side of the same street where a sign still says 'Red Lion Yard'.
11. <u>Cross Keys</u>, 23-30 Red Lion Street a pub from 1620 onwards. It had 8 bedrooms and closed in 1831. It has a Dutch gable and an alley on the north side.
12. <u>Star</u>, further north on the same street.
13. The <u>Fox</u> stood between Sandy Lane, Pound Lane and Fox Lane to the south. It was owned by the Warnes family but only existed in the early to mid-1800s before disappearing without trace.

Appendix (20) <u>Moats in North-East Norfolk</u> – reference, *'Norfolk Archaeology'*, vol 39.

1. <u>Erpingham moats</u> lay north of the church on the east side of the village on the south side of the lane to Alby.
2. <u>Burgh-by-Aylsham</u>, had a gravel platform 25m wide and ditches 3-5m wide. In the 13thc it was held by the royal manor of Cawston. Hubert de Burgh had the right of free warren there, in Aylsham and Buxton.
1281, de Burgh fell into debt and forfeited it to the Crown who granted it to Queen Eleanor. She died in 1291. It had 230 acres of (park?); heath and the Wood Meadow, all valued at £35-2s-9d per annum.
1287, 40 Hanworth oaks were used to enclose the park of Burgh with palings.
1307, more oaks from the Earl of Norfolk's deer park in Hanworth were used to repair the buildings.
1313, the buildings were still in a poor state and £200 was needed to be spent on further repairs. An impressive inventory included;
A great hall, the queen's chamber and chapel; a great chapel, other bed chambers, a watch tower, barns and other farm buildings, a great chamber with 2 guard-robes, a bake house, brew house etc. It was occupied until the late 15th, possibly the early 16thc. Then a farm-house was built 150m to the north-west of the old site. 17 types of 15thc glazed tiles were found on the site as well as Iron Age axe heads and arrows.

3. <u>Great Hautbois Castle</u>,
1313, a license to crenelate was granted to Sir Robert Baynard and his family occupied it until the early 15thc.
1671, the manor contained 176¼ acres. George Batchelor, surveyor of Aylsham listed 9 messuages, 7 cottages, 131 acres arable; 20 acres meadow; 4 acres alder carr and a free fishery in the manor.

Appendix (21) <u>Some of the leading personalities and families of Aylsham</u>.

1. <u>William Ashwell</u>, died in 1457/8 and left a bequest to Aylsham Church – he owned property in the town.
2. <u>Joseph Thomas Clover</u> (1825-82, 57) was born in Aylsham the son of Elizabeth (born, Peterson) and John W. Clover, an Aylsham draper & shop-keeper who married there in 1821. Joseph became a surgeon in 1846 when experiments with anaesthetics began. He was the first full time anaethetists in England. He invented the 'Portable Regulating Inhaler' which was still in general use in London hospitals in 1930. He was a relative of Joseph Clever - a member of the Norwich School of artists who was engaged to an Aylsham lady.
3. <u>Richard Howard</u>; sheriff in 1488, married Margaret the widow of Edward Cutler. Cutler became a Freeman in Norwich 1428, Sheriff in 1453; MP for Norwich 1460-61; and its Mayor in 1470. He and Margaret were both buried in Aylsham Church where their sepulchre brass can still be seen in the north aisle.
4. <u>Thomas Hudson</u>, 1526-58, was condemned by the ruthless John Bury, vicar 1554-58 and Nix, last pre-Reformation Roman Catholic Bishop of Norwich. Hudson was burnt at the stake in during Mary Tudor's reign. 200 people were forced to creep on their knees in penitence towards the altar of Aylsham Church. Bury hit two people in a temper and killed them. He died within days of Queen Mary's death.
5. <u>Robert Jannys</u>, Sheriff in 1509; Mayor 1517 and 1524 and died in 1530. He was born in Aylsham the son of John and Agnes Jannys. He was a wealthy grocer and lived in 2 Ramms House near St George's Church Colegate in Norwich where he was buried – his elaborate terracotta tomb bears the Grocers' Arms. In his Will he left 300 Marks or £10 to pay for a chantry priest to serve in Aylsham Church and to buy land to support a school in Aylsham. He was a friend of Matthew Parker, Archbishop of Canterbury who was born in Norwich a generation earlier. This connection may have led to the foundations of a scholarship for a student from Aylsham in Corpus Christi College, Cambridge. By his wife Margaret he had two daughters. His brother was the priest Sir Thomas Jannys.
6. <u>John Jegon</u> BA, 1550-1618 was a bishop. He lived in Aylsham for four years before dying there aged 67.
7. <u>Christopher Layer</u>, see notes above.
8. <u>Edmund Reeve</u>, 1589-1647, 58. He born in Aylsham the son of Christopher and Marta Reeve; she was the daughter of Edmond Grimston. He was the seneschal (steward) to the Lancaster Manor 1631-39. It was he who drew up the 1622/ 24 list of properties (see below). He was later the Recorder of Great Yarmouth and a Judge of the Common Pleas. His parents moved to Norwich. Christopher died in 1619 leaving seven sons and four daughters.
9. <u>Nicholas Norgate</u> held property in Aylsham such as the tenement in Nether Hall Street. He had relatives in Aylsham though he himself lived in Norwich. He was Mayor in 1564; Sheriff in 1553. In his Will he left money for the teacher's salary in Aylsham School.
10. <u>John Repton</u>, collector of taxes in Norwich bought, 1 The Market Place in 1764. Two of his infants died in 1770, his mother, Martha in 1773. His daughter Dorothy married John Adey who became an Aylsham attorney. John Adey died in 1804. John Repton junior, became a farmer in Oxnead. John's famous son was Humphrey Repton the landscaper. The joint family memorial inside the parish church is a ledger slab in the south aisle of the chancel.
11. Rev <u>Benjamin Suckling</u> (rector of Matlaske 1793-1837) and <u>Horace Suckling</u> were two brothers who lived in Aylsham and were cousins of Lord Nelson.
12. <u>Lancelot Thexton</u> followed John Bury as Vicar but he was a Protestant.
13. Rev <u>Jonathan Wrench</u> was the vicar of Aylsham and he built the Vicarage. He was the son of John Wrench, who was Mayor of Norwich in 1688; and his wife Ann who was the sister of another Mayor, John Rayley in 1649. Jonathan was the younger brother of the famous physician Dr Sir Benjamin Wrench. There are several Wrench ledger slabs in the Sanctuary of Aylsham Church.

<u>Aylsham families</u>

2. <u>The Bulwer family</u>, ref *Burke's Landed Gentry*.
Turold de Dalling was a Norman of Field Dalling, Norfolk. Seven generations later came, John de Dalling who was Lord of the Manor there in 1316. William B, of the same place died in 1775 without issue so his sister Sarah Bulwer (1669-1771) became his heir. She married Rice Wiggett and they had a son, William Wiggett (1730-93). He married in 1756, Mary Earle, of Heydon Hall 1737-98) and inherited there. They had issue; William (a Brigadier General) of Heydon Hall (1757-1807); John (see below), Edward, Frances, Mary, and Sarah.

IMAGE (37) The <u>Rev James Bulwer</u> (1794-1879) MA Cantab, the clergyman and artist who painted scenes of Aylsham etc was the son of **John** and Mary Bulwer (nee, Seaman) and baptised in Aylsham with a sister Elizabeth in 1796. Mrs Bridget Bulwer, lived at Paradise House, Aylsham. His parents owned Aylsham Manor House but James was born in Norwich. He studied in Jesus College, Cambridge and was ordained in 1818. He travelled to Ireland, Portugal, Madeira and returned to Bristol; then London where he was friendly with the Norfolk artist Miles Edmund Cotman. They both had antiquarian interests and painted topographical images. Cotman's father was John Sell Cotman who may have taught painting to Bulwer. He was a curate in Aylsham between 1840-48 after which he went to Hunworth where he remained. He was the librarian at Blickling Hall and in 1869 he was instrumental in allowing experts to study the rare Anglo-Saxon book, called the '*Blickling Homilies*'.

The Bulwer estate.
The Rev James Bulwer is shown above. In April 1816, a survey was made of his estate in Aylsham; NRO BR 276/1/0941. The 1875 edition of '*Burkes Landed Classes*' says he lived in Hunworth, Nfk and held about 300 acres (in Aylsham?). The Bulwer family of Heydon had nearly 8,000 acres.

3.   The Copeman family.
<u>Richard Copeman</u> (born 1711) married Susannah Breese (born 1716) of Aylsham (his portrait by J. Zoffany RA). Their son was;
<u>Robert Copeman</u>, senior; (1740-1803) was steward to the Earl of Buckinghamshire. He married Katherine Turner and bought the Old Bank, on the corner of Burgh and Norwich Roads in Aylsham in 1800 -1801, plus 23 acres near Spratts Green. He lived in London House which stood on the site of the later Town Hall. It faced southwards directly onto the Market Place so its elegant sashed windows were provided with shutters! His portrait was painted by J. Northcote RA. Katherine Copeman was Lord of Aylsham Woods Manor in 1818. Their son was;
<u>Robert Copeman</u>, junior. (1769-18..) He was a solicitor, JP and Steward from 1794 onwards. He was licensed to issue bank notes in 1815. In 1817 there were only 17 banks in the whole of Norfolk. He lived at the sumptuous West Lodge in Aylsham with its spacious grounds and rich herbaceous borders. From 1815 he was an attorney, and also a banker after being licensed in 1822. There was a strong room in his cellars to store the bank's gold sovereigns. He was succeeded by his sons;
<u>George and Thomas Copeman</u> – the latter lived in Bank House. In 1855 they sold the business to Gurneys Bank of Norwich having issued notes worth £ 5,864.

4, <u>Doughty family of Hanworth and Aylsham</u>. Early Doughtys – *Harleian Society* vol 32, p108. Same Arms for both branches.
          1552, '*Visitation to Norfolk by the College of Heralds*'.
Thomas – Elizabeth, dau of John Houghton, sister of Sir Robert Houghton, had issue'
Robert (buried in Aylsham, 1621) – mar Sarah daughter of Thomas Bramsby of Poringland, Nfk; issue

1. **Robert** (died 1679) – mar 1639,	2. William (died 1686) of Aylsham mar 1664
Katherine dau of Roger Townsend	Frances dau of John Durrant of Aylsham
Issue;	

1. William   6. Katherine
2. Robert   7. John, 1644- 1702. He married Elizabeth, who died by 1684
3. Sarah   8. ? Barbara, Mrs Parker
4. Ann
          See notes about Robert Doughty junior, below.
          other members of the family;
          Thomas Doughty was in a legal dispute with the Vicar of Aylsham over the tithes of Horstead?
          It was settled with payments made in the south porch of Aylsham Church as was the custom.
          Other Doughtys who were buried in Aylsham Church;
      Robert Doughty 1612; Ann his wife 1612; William Doughty 1646; Thomas Doughty 1660; Anne his wife
          1671; Robert Doughty 1679.
<u>Major Robert Doughty</u> was a Major in the Norfolk Regiment of Foot serving Parliament under Sir John Hobart of Blickling. In 1639 he married Katherine Townsend in Norwich, a cousin of Lord Townsend. At the end of the Commonwealth he became the secretary and right-hand man to Mr Paston of Oxnead Hall whose family's political allegiances had leaned in the opposite direction to Doughty's during the Civil War. Doughty

took up residence in Oxnead and under the Restoration he seemed to be thriving. This continued up to the death of his father in 1679. At the same time his son John Doughty had been indiscrete in Norwich about Paston's affairs so it was time for Robert to move on. He went to Barbados as secretary to the governor Sir Richard Duff and in 1683 he became the solicitor-general there.

5. <u>The tree of the Norgate family of Aylsham</u>. *Norfolk Genealogy*, vol 13, 118-124.
    Alexander de Norgate, of Cawston? Living,1327, issue;
1. Nicholas, 18 Edward II   2. Adam, 23 Edward II, issue;
1. Rev John, rector of Ingworth 1408 and other places later. 2. Robert, of Swanton Abbot, Nfk, issue;
Robert, married Priscilla, issue
Robert (?) issue;
1. John Norgate of Aylsham, MA Cantab, born c1510; one of the town's wealthiest residents, mar (1) Alice Bulwer of Dalling; mar (2) Alice Howard, issue;
    1. Anthony, of Aylsham, apprenticed as an overseas merchant in 1553, died 1594; mar Rachel Thompson, issue;
        John, Robert, Anthony, William, Mary, Alice, Cicely
    2. Robert MA, DD, Master of Corpus Christi College, Cambridge; mar Elizabeth Baker, died 1587.
    3. Henry, of Aylsham, NCC Will proved 1619; mar Anne Gaultly, issue;
        1. Thomas (given a lease in Aylsham in 1611) 2. Henry, at school in Aylsham, then Cambridge.
        3. Mary, born c1595
    4. Nicholas
    5. Rev William Norgate, MA Cantab 1597 rector of Panfield, Essex; died 1619.
2. Thomas, bn 1513,3. Henry of Cawston, died 1541; 4. Cecily. 5. Mrs Holland 6. Nicholas, gent owner of the Maids Head Hotel, Norwich.

6. The <u>Wrench family</u> arrived in Aylsham with the new vicar, Jonathan in 1700. Jonathan Wrench (1667-1741, 74) was at Norwich Grammar School; Caius College Cambridge in 1685; a scholar in 1686; BA 1689; MA 1693. He was the Rector of Burgh-by-Aylsham, between 1704-1740, as well as Vicar of Aylsham. His brother was Sir Benjamin Wrench, MD of Norwich; one of the city's famous doctors. His son Jonathan Wrench, junior (1703-65, 62) was also a priest.

7. The <u>Soame family</u> farmed in Aylsham from the 16th century onwards and supplied many church-wardens to the parish. Some of their memorials are in the north transept of the church. The Soame Pump was donated by John Soame Austen in memory of is uncle, John Soame (1834-1910) and opened at a public ceremony held there on 29 May 1913. Old cottages were demolished on the site before the open shelter, thatched with Norfolk Reed was built. This is at the junction of Cawston, Pinfold and Blickling Roads.

8. The <u>Purdy family</u> of Woodgate House. These included Robert John Woods W Purdy, 1839-1916; Lt Col Thomas Woods Purdy, 1873-1960 who bought Aylsham Woods Manor; Capt Thomas Purdy, 1909- ; and his son, Peter Purdy. The family originated from Houghton and Kelling but the name also occurs in early records of Aylsham. The son of Aylsham historian, Dr John Ireland Sapwell married into this family.

9. The <u>Parmenter family</u>.
Robert Parmenter (1) He died in 1791 and was succeeded by his son,
Robert Parmenter (2) 1764-1831,
Robert Parmenter (3) 1794- 1880, 86. He was a solicitor who took over the management of the town's water mill. In 1822 he became the Deputy Steward of the Manor. He married Sarah Churchill. They lived at 'Paremter's House' on the east side of Cromer Road where he and his wife Sarah added a Georgian front to Clyde House 1823 onwards. The original small house is shown on the 1839 Tithe Map set back from the road. There was a house on the same site in 1598. It was rebuilt with a Dutch gable in 1677. It was briefly used as a Vicarage.

A selection of large Aylsham houses and their families.

1. Abbot's Hall, was owned in 1610 by Robert Wood Lord of the Manor who built it on the site of Abbot Sampson's medieval and moated manor house.
   Abbott's Hall (no 2) was built in the 18thc by John Peterson and later the home of the Shepheard family.

IMAGE (38)

2. Aylsham Old Hall, (left) on Blickling Lane was built by a member of the Windham family of Felbrigg Hall in 1686-9. It was occupied by Robert Copeman, agent of the 2nd Earl of Buckingham after the Blickling Estate acquired it in 1751.

IMAGE (39)

3. Bank House, (left) 3 Norwich Road, with Angel Close it covered 5½ acres.

4. Bayfield House, north end of Red Lion Street.

5. Belt Lodge, is a cottage where the front part of its roof is thatched. It lies on the corner of Sir William's Lane and Gas House Hill. The Belt estate dates from the 1600s. It was the home of the milling family of Parmenter.

IMAGE (40)

6. Bolwick Hall, (left) was owned by the Warnes family. It is a Georgian mansion set in a small park with a lake and water mill on the south side. One member of the family was Mayor of Norwich in the late 1400s.

IMAGE (41)

7. Bure House, (shown left) in Millgate was owned by Robert Palmer, the manager of the water mill.
9. Bridge House, Millgate – converted to a pub in the late 1800s.
10. Bushy House, Cromer Road built in 1855; Dr Richard Morton, owner; later a private school.

110

IMAGE (42)

8. Black Boys Hotel, may originally have been a house but it was recorded as a pub in 1659. Daniel Defoe, Parson Woodforde and Lord Nelson (who had relatives in the town) visited it. It had a stable for 40 horses, 3 ostlers and 4 post boys. The entry to the yard at the centre was blocked up in the 1930s. It had a cock-pit and an assembly room where 200 people could gather. The central square balcony was replaced by a modern half-round one. On the north side is a shaped brick gable.

11. Collegiate House, Mill Road

12. Dye's House, on the west side of the Market Place. It has a timbered frame and a Medieval cellar. It was converted into offices but now is a house again.

13. The Grange, Cromer Road east side – it was once the home of the eminent Aysham historian, Dr Sapwell.

14. The Gothic House, Hungate used as a girl's school in the 19thc.

15. Holman House, north side of the Market Place facing the churchyard. Regency red brick 2 storeys with sash windows. It has a medieval under-croft so built on an earlier house. Thomas Cooke was one of its owners.

16. Knoll House, School House Lane, off Blickling Road, opposite the school. It had the Old Bowling Green shown on the Tithe Map. It has 18thc panelling inside.

17. London House, on the north side of the Market Place. The eastern half was included in the Corn Hall, built in 1857. When it became Town Hall the building was extended westwards to include the rest of London House.

18. Maltings, now converted into a number of dwellings – on the west side of Mill Gate. On the wall, 'R. Parmenter 1781'.

19. Manor House, on the corner of Norwich Road and Burgh Road.

16. 1 Market Place; three storeys high with a fine pedimented doorway. Originally there were bollards in front of it. This was the home of the Repton family and later, of John Adey the attorney.

17. Orchard House opposite the old Manor House on Norwich Road. William Repton lived there in 1848. It was rebuilt in the late 19thc in half timbered, mock-Tudor style and is now divided into flats. It was built around the clock in 8 hour shifts, with 'great lights' used at night.

20. Old Bank House, on the corner of Norwich and Burgh Roads. Built in the early 17thc it became Copeman's

Bank in the early 18thc until it was taken over by larger banks which are still located close by.

21. 'Paradise House', west of the church.

22. Repton House, in a loke by the southern churchyard gate.

IMAGE (43)

23. Old Vicarage, (shown left) 1700-1956, north of the churchyard built by Jonathan Wrench; 7 x 2½ bays with former glebe land attached to it. Testimony – Mr Thexton (son of the parson?) was a shop-keeper, related to the Barker family of whom there were many in Aylsham.

IMAGE (44)

24. West Lodge (left) set in five acres of grounds including a large kitchen garden. An impressive 3 storeys, Georgian house built perhaps by the Marquis of Townsend for one of his mistresses.

25. The Wilding, north-east of the church near Dye's Loke

26. Woodgate House, west of the town (see above).

Map (33) <u>some of the occupants of the Town centre in 1839.</u>

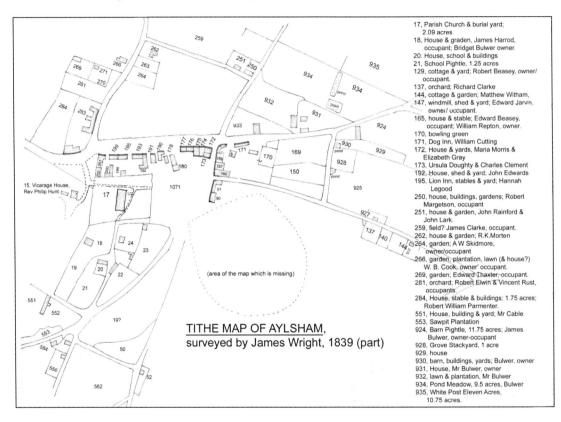

17, Parish Church & burial yard;
2.09 acres
18, House & graden, James Harrod,
occupant; Bridget Bulwer owner.
20. House, school & buildings
21, School Pightle, 1.25 acres
129, cottage & yard; Robert Beasey, owner/
occupant.
137, orchard; Richard Clarke
144, cottage & garden; Matthew Witham,
owner/ occupant.
147, windmill, shed & yard; Edward Jarvis,
occupant.
165, house & stable; Edward Beasey,
occupant; William Repton, owner.
170, bowling green
171, Dog Inn, William Cutting
172, House & yards, Maria Morris &
Elizabeth Gray
173, Ursula Doughty & Charles Clement
192, House, shed & yard; John Edwards
195, Lion Inn, stables & yard; Hannah
Legood
250, house, buildings, gardens; Robert
Margetson, occupant
251, house & garden, John Rainford &
John Lark.
259, field? James Clarke, occupant.
262, house & garden; R.K.Morten
264, garden; A W Skidmore,
owner/occupant
266, garden, plantation, lawn (& house?)
W. B. Cook, owner' occupant.
269, garden; Edward Thaxter, occupant.
281, orchard; Robert Elwin & Vincent Rust,
occupants.
284, House, stable & buildings; 1.75 acres;
Robert William Parmenter.
551, House, building & yard; Mr Cable
553, Sawpit Plantation
924, Barn Pightle, 11.75 acres; James
Bulwer, owner-occupant.
928, Grove Stackyard, 1 acre
929, house
930, barn, buildings, yards; Bulwer, owner
931, House, Mr Bulwer, owner
932, lawn & plantation, Mr Bulwer
934, Pond Meadow, 9.5 acres, Bulwer
935, White Post Eleven Acres,
10.75 acres.

15. Vicarage House,
Rev Philip Hunt

TITHE MAP OF AYLSHAM,
surveyed by James Wright, 1839 (part)

(area of the map which is missing)

112

PAGE ONE;	Acres		Acres
Edward Mayes, pasture	2½	James Gogle, market stall	10'x 5'
Edward Rye, 2 market stalls	8'x 4'	same, tenement with garden	4P
John Watson, cott & garden	10 P	John Hand; pasture	5
Agnes Aldridge, stall	-	Edmund Watts; in Starmancroft	3
Kath Scarboro, tenement in	½	same; messuage, 2 barns, etc by	
Netherhall St, yard & well		Le Backside in the market place	7/8
Henry Woodrow; messuage,	12 P	same; part of 12 acres.	6
tenement, garden & orchard.		same; Parsons Close.	2
same; a messuage; land in Fussils	¼	same; land with a ditch	2
Close on Blickling Road.		same; 2 lands	3½
Robert Bateman, a close	12	Tho Coates, 3 lands in Stonegate	3½
same; pasture/ arable	2½	same; land in Heathcroft	5
same; a messuage & barn	¾	same; 3 pieces of 3, 3 & ¾ acres	6¾
heath	¾	same; a close	1½
land	3	same; more lands in Stonegate	3¾
William Tompson; mess & garden	¼	same; 5 parts in 2 pieces in same	9
James Bell; Wall Croft	15	same; Suckling Close with ditches	2¼
same; a meadow	2	same; part of 5 pieces	2¼
Rev Thomas Munday; Hobbes		same; messuage, barn & stable	
Tenement with barn, orchard &		taken from woodland	16
close on Hungate Street.	2	same; taken from heath-land	1½
same; Bunnes pasture	3	same; a toft with barn, cottage,	
same; a market stall	-	garden, close	2¾
same; Le Furr Close in the heath	20	Thomas Halifax; messuage, barn,	
same; 8 parts of a messuage	1/8	stable, in the market place.	½
Robert Alleyn; messuage of stable,		same; Leoland	½
close & garden on Easten Green.	3	same; Le Tiled Toft – house & gdn	20 P
same; Le Gravill Close	4	same; tenement in market place	-
another close	9	same; Back House - an office.	-
Red Fen messuage	¾	Lancelot Thexton; messuage, hay	
Richard Thompson, tenement at the		house, stable, barn & buildings	¼
great bridge	7P	same; a market stall.	7' x 4'
John Brady; land - end of Hungate	¾	same; a close	7
another	¾	Robert Tompson, a tenement	10 P
another	2	Humphrey Holby; arable/ pasture	1¾
heath land	¾	same; arable/ pasture, a close	5
land in two pieces	3	same; messuage with yard	1/8
another in two pieces	4	same; messuage in Stonegate on	
pasture	1/8	the Back Way; barn; pasture.	10
Robert Coye; a market stall	2 P	same; meadow	1
William Baker; Chamberalin's	2	another meadow	1½
Little Close; same – meadow	3	same; 2 lands by Cawston Road	2
same, 2 storey shop & 2 storey		same; 2 closes in West Field	7
cabin next to it by the		same; half a stall in the market.	6' x ?
Market + 2 rooms & a yard.	8 P	same; Marsham Gap Pightle	2¾
John Jones, shop in Marketstead	7' x10'	same; mess with meadow &	
James Gogle; messuage of a garden	-	pasture adjoining StoneGate.	10
same, part of a garden	¼	same; land in East Field	1
same, cottage in a ¼ messuage all	-	same; ½ messuage; garden & orch	½
in Hungate Street.		same; land in East Field	1
same, a market stall	8' x 5'	same; shop in the market place	10' x ?

	Acres		Acres
Humphrey Holby		same; a toft in Stonegate.	2
same; a ditched piece of land	2½	same; Cobbs Close	14
a long planted piece	½	same; land in Stonegate.	3
a messuage in Market Street	20 P	same; Priests Meadow	1½
Lancelot Thaxton; a ditched pightle		same; a close in East Field Robert	11
with a new barn.	3/8	& Richard Swann, tenement	¼
same; a ditched close.	1	with an orchard.	
same; close in West Field.	2½	James Smith; lands in various uses.	124
Gregory Breuiter, messuage , barn,		same; Larwood Yard in Hungate.	½
stable, malt house, gardens &		same; various parcels.	11
orchard & close.	14	same; market fish stall.	5' x 3'
same; Dovehouse Close	2	Robert Gurney; messuage - cottage,	
same; parcels of meadow &		orchard and garden in Millgate.	¼
pasture in East Field.	49	same; messuage; yard & pightle.	¾
John Breuiter; closes of arable/ past	21	Simon Leverington; messuage	17 P
Robert Rump, a messuage of barn,		same; house, out-house, garden,	
stables, orchard, garden & land		close with a barn in Hungate.	7/8
in Washing Yard.	1½	same; plot in the market place.	7' x 4'
same, enclosed parcels.	4	same; land.	3
same; parcels of pasture abutting		same; land in the (Common) Field	3¼
Cawston Lane	6½	same; in the same field, south.	½
same; parcels in 3 acres.	1	same; another small piece.	2 P
Robert & wife, Martha Baker;		same; land by a road.	2½
parcels of arable etc.	26	same; close in West Field.	6
part of a heath	1	same; Fur Ground Close by Jarvis	
another piece of heath.	1	Bridge Wood.	6
William Scottow – land in Scottow	-	same; heath	10 P
Lawrence Barr, in Carr Ground	½	same; land in Hungate.	6
another piece in the same.	½	John Youngs; in Cobb's Close	3
Robert Doughty, a messuage with		same; cottage with backside.	½
barn, buildings, a chantrey,		same; pasture.	2
woodhouse, orchard & backside		same; heath in Stonegate Heath.	¾
in the Old Market of Aylsham;	2	same; more in the same heath.	2
same; scattered pieces of land.	40¼	Thomas Lawes, messuage with	
same; pasture.	1/8	orchard & garden.	2
same; pasture in Cockerell Field.	4	same; 4 market stalls.	-
same; Fayles Toft	7	same; Palmersdale Close.	6
same; Pyes Close.	7	same; a close by Brandledike.	3
Thomas Knowles, heath close	10	same; Hungate Close.	2
same; in Little Close by the Church		same; land in West Field	5
Gate leading to the Old Market.	2	same; land in Market Field.	1
Chris Sankey; a house & shop.	14' x8'	same; Tudmore Close in mixed use	15
same; a market stall.	8' x 6'	same; garden & parcel in Hungate	¼
Simon Smith; a messuage with		Thomas Smith; messuage, 2 cotts,	
barn & buildings.	1	barn & garden in Hungate	2
same; parcels of land arable/ past.	70½	same; half of a decayed messuage	
same, West Yard in Stonegate	1	in Moorgate, meadow & pasture.	60
same; meadow in Norgate	1	same; a messuage in Churchyard.	10 P
same; decayed stall in the market	8' x 4'	Edward Brampton; a messuage by	
same; land	1	the river in 7 parts.	80¼
same; messuage & a yard.	¼		

	Acres		Acres
Edward Brampton contin'd;		same; ungoverned heath near	
a strip of land 60' x 12'/ 3'	1/8	Cawston Bridge.	2
same; parcels of land.	8	same; land.	15
same; more	28	same; land	3/8
same; more; in Whittenharm.	1	same; heath by Cawston Park	¾
same; more in 2 pieces. East Field.	2½	same; heath	1
same; more	1½	same; part of a close	3
same; more in 2 pieces	1¼	John Josterhus & Peter Barker	
same; more	2½	land.	2
same; more in Cookes land	2½	same, a close.	9
same; 3 pieces in Smalden	1½	same, land	¾
same; 3 more lands in Bean Land	2	same, a land	2
same; messuage	18	same, land	1
same; Backhouse Pasture, 2 virgates.	60?	same; Suckling Meadow	3¾
same; close.	8	same; Sturmans Meadow	12P
same; Read Fenn marsh	2	same, Feanters Messuage Close	12
same; a land in East Field.	2	same; Gott's Messuage	16½
William & wife, Christina Orwell,		same; Wicket's Close heath land	3
a ditched land.	¾	same; tenement.	2
same; more land.	2	same; tenement with a shed	1/8
same; Paradise tenement, barn.	2¼	same; shop, 2 stalls, barn & back.	1
same; Courts Close	2	John & wife, Elizabeth Reymes,	
same; messuage with passage.	4	Chamberlayn's Tenement with	
same; a close.	7	meadow & garden in Stonegate.	2
same; Smiths Close	17	George Soute, Millbourne Close.	6½
same; land in the same close.	3	same; messuage, stable, cellar,	
same; ditto.	½	yard.	¼
same; land	¼	same; Cuboard Lyng.	¾
same; land in Chosley Croft	2	William Harper; tenement in	
same; 2 pieces in the next croft.	1	Hungate Street.	10P
same; land 17 yards x 10'/ 8'.	-	Francis Eastow, messuage	1½
same; Overdey Messuage.	¼	same, land part of 120 acres.	33½
same; Wickets Tenement in the		same, heath.	1
middle of Aylsham.	-	same; land	1
same; a messuage west of the		same; pasture in Market Field.	3
market; buildings, barn, gardens.	1	same; 2 closes.	7
same; hemp-land & backside.	26 P	same; small yard in mixed use.	9
William Orwell; a croft.	11	William Fisher; ½ tenement, shop	
same; Reeds Close	12	& yard	11P
same; pieces of land in 2 closes.	10½	same; he other half.	11 P
same; heath.	12	Richard Wilson, Market Field land	1
same; land	14	same; land in East Field.	½
same; messuage barn & garden in		same; built up tenement.	¾
Woodgate Street.	1	same; another in Millgate.	1
same; arable land in the Field.	15	same; heath in Sir William's	1¼
same; land.	1	same; more land.	1¼
same; messuage with land.	1½	Thomas Cressy, Angel messuage,	
same; land in 3 pieces	1¼	barn & yard.	2½
same; pasture	16	same; Ollands	11
same; more arable	1¾	same; Fir Ground	2
same; land	1		

PAGE FOUR	Acres		Acres.
Thomas Cressy, contin'; Greys Messuage + meadow & pasture.	8	John Orwell junior; John Barker junior, Thomas Halifax, Simon Cressey etc; 2 almshouses on the way to Marsham.	-
same; messuage with hemp yard in Millgate Street; 12 inhabitants	1¾	Richard Smith, Heath Close.	35
same; Wilst's land.	3¼	same, a close by Cocksrowshut.	5
same; Paysons Land by Fair Stead	1¼	same, a close by Kings Green.	6
same; Fair Stead on Olland.	¼	same, close in Cookdale.	12
John Breuiter, Jelions Rood	10	same, 2 parts of Fir Close	30
same; Thorofare Close.	7	John Orwell, the grist & malt mills with a toft & stable	-
same; Broomscroft.	3	Thomas Clare, shop & well in a long yard in Hungate Street.	-
William Uniper, market stall	7' x 7'	Edward –Edmund Reve, the Steward, in Old Market St. with a barn.	1
Margaret Chosell, messuage, brew & back house, other buildings, a close & yard.	2	same, Stone House Pightle	1
same, land by the Dam	1	same, a close between 2 others.	2
same, built up shop in the market.	10' x8'	same, messuage with barn, stables for 3 horses & a brewhouse.	1
same; butcher's stall	40'x ?	same, tenement & cottage	1
same, arable land in pieces	13	same, cottage 24 x 29 rods.	-
same, arable in 2 pieces	5	same, toft with a decayed antique cottage in the Old Market.	2½
same; heath land	7	same, Marshalls Messuage built up	½
same, more heath	3	same, lands in closes	3
same, close by the highway	7	same, toft & ruined messuage	1½
same; arable land	½	same, messuage & toft	½
same, built up shop	12' x7'	same, ditched messuage.	¼
same, arable land in West Field	12'x12'	same, enclosed land	¾
same, 2 closes, mixed uses.	3¼	John Barker, barns, messuage in Church Gate Street.	2
same, arable land in a close	20	same, another messuage.	½
same, more arable.	1¾	same, meadow & pasture in Woodgate.	13
same, more arable in West Field	¾	Joanna Day, Saffron Ground	½
same, arable in a close, East Field	1/8	William Kymer, meadow.	3
same, market stall	3	same, in a 2½ acre close.	½
same, arable in East Field	24' x ?	same, 20 % of a messuage.	16P
same, close	1	same, tenement with barn & stables for 2 in Eastern Street.	3
same, house, orchard, garden (former shop)	2	same, arable land in 2 pieces and a pightle in the same street.	¾
same, former shop which burnt	20 P	same, more land	3¾
same, messuage by Wills Egge with barn	20' x ?	same, more in Eastern Field by the main road, from Kettle-bridge to Brampton.	8½
same, arable land	¼	same, a decayed messuage.	1
same, cottage, pightle in East Field	2½	Elizabeth Kymer, arable land.	2½
same, mixed use in 2 parts.	¼	same, 1/5 th part of a messuage on the east side of the church.	-
same, built up shop in the market	1		
same, close in pasture.	12' x ?		
same, arable land in 3 closes.	6		
same; barn & close	6		
same, waste land	3		
same, Waggstaffe tenement.	8' x 7'		
Robert Geagan, John Orwell, Robert Doughty etc; School House with Paradise Close south.	¼ 2		

Description	Acres	Description	Acres
Elizabeth Kymer, continued;		same, land in Westgate Field.	1¼
1/5th of a market place shop	-	same, messuage, orchard & pasture	2
Edward Whitmore, plot in the		same, a pightle	1½
market place.	10'x10'	same, Woolcross Shop	27'x27'
Alicia Homes, cottage + a 10' Yard.	8 P	same, Hobart Pightle	1
Joanna Akers, ½ a tenement.	4P	same, heath in 2 parts	1½
Robert Thompson, tenement.	½	Alice Reymer, tenement in	
Robert & wife Anna Wood;		Hungate Street	4P
Bolwick Manor, 2 barns, stables,		same, land opposite over the road.	1½
other buildings, pasture.	8½	same, land in various pieces.	12
same, arable, woods, pasture,		Emma Smythe, land	1¾
heath, marsh.	42	Rachell Norgate, Boy Messuage, a	
same, arable land etc	46	yard in the Market Place	20P
same, land in Bolwick Field once		same, cott & garden by a Pinfold	10P
in 7 pieces.	6	Robert Gelle, messuage, barn,	
same, 2 pieces in Skipping Croft	5	Smith's Shop, barn, orchard.	1
same, 5 pieces in Bolwick Field.	3½	Elizabeth Wadlow, tenement.	13P
same, land in East Field	1½	William Moore, market stall.	12' by?
same, land	2	Robert Curtis, arable in East Field.	4
same, Manor of Calys messuage	3/8	Thomas Harwood, barn & close.	3
same, lands in mixed use.	82	same, arable land in North Croft.	¾
same, meadow.	20	same, more arable.	2½
same, arable.	2	Nicholas Brady, arable land &	
same, meadow.	1	cottage in Hungate'	4
same, meadow.	1¼	same, close.	1
same, part of a meadow.	½	same, arable land in Palmers Dale	½
John Pye, cottage.	½	same, land in pieces in Hungate	4½
Robert Harmer, market stall	7' x 4'	Gregory Whissiter, a stall.	12'x12'
William Harmer, of Sheyfield;		same, another stall.	6' x 4'
butchers stall in the market	30'x30'	same, a pightle.	1
Peter Empson, part of a shop	-	same, another pightle	½
Thomas & wife Emma Leoman;		Edward Allen, Dowes Messuage	
messuage in Stonegate; barn,		with barn	2
stables, out-houses, gardens,		same, arable land in many place	20
orchards.	2½	same, messuage plus a close	2
same, Messuage, mill house, brew		same, arable pightle	1¼
house, croft & little pightle.	10½	same, arable close	4
same, parcel	16¾	same, orchard tenement	1
same, parcel of arable.	4	William Corker,	
same, land with 2 cottages &		a plot almost in the market	15'x12'
meadow in Stonegate.	2	William Green,	
same, parcel in 10 Acre Close.	3½	a tenement with a back	¾
same, built up messuage with		Robert & wife Christina Bussell,	
stable & yard.	2½	Wattercroft Close	16
same, land.	1¼	same, Little Yard in the	
same, land	3	Workhouse Tenement	6P
same, Seven Acres Close	7	same, cottage & access to well	¼
same, Apple Heath Close	4	Rowland Turner, cottage & back.	20P
same, Candle Close	1½	Chris Cressey, heathland	1½
same, part of Crowdale	¼	same, mixed use land	2
same, cottage	¼	same, tenement with barn & back	¼

PAGE SIX	Acres		Acres
Chris Cressey, continued		Mildred & Martha Baker, a market	
land with a barn	2	stall & 1/3rd of a messuage.	6P
same, orchard & buildings	30'x170'	same, parcels of land in the Fields.	1½
Thomas Norgate, parts of a land	4	John Durrant,	
same, part of 9 acres in		A shop in the market place.	2P
Sturman's Close	3	Thomas Richard & James Smith,	
same, 3 lands in West Field	2	3 pieces of heath	1¼
same, 2 others in Sturmans	3½	Same; another piece of heath.	½
same, ditto	½	John Soame, land & a barn	¼
same, 5 pieces of land	6	Thomas Puttock, mess & garden	1
same, Homestall, Hills Barn,		same, land in Willsegg	15¼ 8P
stable in Old Market Street	4	same, land next to Howards Close	6¼
same, Sillcroft	3	same, a close in Crofto Mess	2
same, parcel of land	1	same, land at end of Willsegg	¾
same, various pieces	9½	same, pasture	3¼
same, Hill's Close	5	same, land in East Field	5/8
same, messuage with land	1	same, another	3/8
same, another 26 virgates long	?	same, 3 pightles in a new close	½
same, mess with a garden & land	¼	same,,in East Field	5½
same, another	½	land in Hungate	6 + 3/8
same, part of 8 Acres, West Field	2½	same, another	3/8
same. part of Sturmans Close	9½	Joanna Haund,	
Margaret Chosell, barn, stable,	3	tenement in the Old Market	1/8
same, arable land in Sturmans	¾	Margaret & John Furmary, garden	10P
same, mixed use, Brundale Ditch	1¼	Ann Thurston, shop, barn, work-	
same, meadow/ pasture	3½	house, garden.	1/8
Thomas Empson, mess +buildings	½	Robert Rayner, Market shop	18' x1'?
John Prick, built up tenement in the		same, a loke.	18' x 6'
market place, house & shop, stable,		Nicholas Brady, land in Fir Ground	
yard, garden.	1/8	on Apple Heath.	¾
same, stable with flat over it.	1/8	Jacob Raynor, cottage & back.	10P x2P
Henry Soame, barn with meadow,		Joanna Elles, cottage & orchard.	32P
heath & pasture in Woodgate.	38	Sir Charles Cornwallis, the manor	
same, 2 land in Stonegate.	9	house & gate house, stable, 3 yards,	
same, part of a land	1	orchard, garden, hop yard.	4
same, another	1	same, meadow closes.	20
same, part of a 3 acre land	1	same, arable closes	112
same, land near the roadway	4	same, pasture closes.	100
same, another	1¼	John Orwell, a messuage in	
same, another	½	Millgate Street	¼
John Soane, arable, heath, pasture	27	same, meadows	54¼,20P
William & wife Joan Kirby,		same, a land	1
messuage with orchard	¾	same, land in the Field.	2
Richard Tompson, tents & orchard.	1¼	Edward & George Pettus, hold	
Same, pasture	¾	several lands free so not listed.	?
John Cobb, 3 cottages with		(All those listed below were	
tenement, orchard & garden	2	outside Aylsham)	
Robert & wife Margaret Foster,		Edmund Haund, land in 3 pieces.	2
Cockerill Field; arable.	2	same, land in Skornerstone.	2
same, part of Parson's Close.	2	Thomas Edwards, Pattinstile Close	
Alice Godfrey, tenement.	20' x ?	north of Scottow glebe.	-

PAGE SEVEN			
same, other lands in Scottow.	-	Abbreviations;	
John Warnes, customary land.	½	P = perches/ 5½ yards in length.	
Edmund Moulton, land in Scottow.	-	5/8 = 2.5 roods.	
Robert Spendlove, in Scottow.	-		
Peter & wife Dorothy Welles	1/8		
Chris Tallis, Skeyton Field land.	-		
William Woodrow, land in same	-		
William Church, ditto.	-		
Thomas Allen, land in Marsham.	-		
Agneta Walker, in Hevingham.	-		
James Gedge, lands in the same.	-		
Agnes Horne, built up messuage in Marsham.	1		
John Warnes, land in same.	2		
Agnes Black, Clark House in Knott's Tenement with land in Marsham.	1		
William Lubbock in Scottow. END	2¾		
Total area in Aylsham, listed above;	---------	2,443¾ acres	

IMAGE (45) Bank Street - the south side of Aylsham Market Place c1870, with three grand Georgian town houses. The left had one was occupied by William Repton, attorney; the middle one became Gurneys Bank. Both once had impressive doorways (one survives) and bollards on the roadside instead of kerbs. Older and more traditional shops are shown on the extreme left; and right at the corner of Hungate Street.

IMAGE (46) Next page - an imaginary reconstruction of the interior of Aylsham Parish Church in the early 1500s with its Roman Catholic fittings, soon to be dismantled by the reformers. Anne Boleyn would have been about eight years old then. There were two Earls of Ormond at this time so it is uncertain whether this image shows her father. Archbishop Matthew Parker, a Norwich man says that Anne was born in Norfolk but she is unlikely to have visited Aylsham and Blickling after she went abroad in 1511.

The Reverend Thomas Tyson shows the Earl of Wiltshire and his daughter, Anne Boleyn of Blickling the newly completed screen in Aylsham Church, in 1508.